About the Author

Saeed was born in Jordan, Amman. He showed interest in writing from a young age. His interests have always been in history and philosophy, and his life based on innovation, challenge and giving, is filled with hobbies that renew the spirit with optimism and positivity. One of his most important values is the creation and development of new ways of thinking and living; that's what he thinks people need the most: personalistic visions and values based on challenge and intellectual flexibility.

Be a Liar
From Negativity to Positivity

Saeed Qahwaji

Be a Liar
From Negativity to Positivity

Olympia Publishers
London

www.olympiapublishers.com
OLYMPIA PAPERBACK EDITION

A CIP catalogue record for this title is
available from the British Library.

ISBN: 978-1-78830-574-7

First Published in 2020

Olympia Publishers
Tallis House
2 Tallis Street
London
EC4Y 0AB

Printed in Great Britain

Acknowledgements

Thanks to all the efforts that have helped to bring out this book and special thanks to:

Hasan Ramaha, my friend and uncle at the same time, for his great support.

Lawrence Daham and Rasha Zaghloul, for their positive support in a negative environment.

Contents

Introduction

When I completed writing this book, I was perplexed because I had not consulted any person concerning the topic it discusses. One night when four of my friends and I met at one of their houses, I decided to disclose the book and find out their views about the type of lying that I wanted to deliver and clarify to the general public.

Whilst we were together, I said, "I want to tell you something important, guys. I have composed a new book, but it is on a completely different topic. It is on a topic nobody has ever approached the way I have."

After I finished speaking I found that neither of them had heard one single word; they were arguing and talking about things I did not think worthy of bringing up. I repeated what I had said, louder this time, and fortunately they paid attention.

Then one of them asked, "Alright, what's that topic you need to convey that no person has ever discussed the way you have?"

I replied, "I discuss lying."

"We don't get you."

"What I mean is that the book discusses lying, and it urges people to be liars."

"Do you mean that you're encouraging readers to be liars?" one of them asked.

"That's right."

One of them laughed and said, "Guys, we haven't met here today to talk about unrealistic stuff."

Another contended, "OK. Let's not mess up the night we've been waiting months for."

I did not speak any more. All I was trying to do that night was to find an approach to convey my idea or at least, to find a way to save myself from that trouble. Since I was aware of the human nature that does not understand or accept complete change in some topics that we consider as negative, I was prepared to wait for a long time. Most people do not enjoy sufficient mental flexibility that enables them to see things wisely from a wider, broader perspective; they perceive things from a narrow perspective because they are imprisoned within the fence of their primitive ideas.

Then the one sitting next to me boldly said, "Let's discuss it in a more mature way than we already have." He went on to ask me, "You're now talking about the importance of lying?"

"That's right."

"Alright, if what you're saying is correct, do you think there'll be a publisher that accepts publishing your book?"

The one in front of me said, "OK, this was exactly what I wanted to say."

At this point I replied, "I can understand your feelings, but it's another type of lying; it's different from lying that occurred to you. It is positive lying, or a positive lying tool used at times of adversity, to help us enjoy a flexible mentality that elevates us to the highest level of power and intelligence. The book will show how people use various versions of this type of lying. It'll disclose the biggest negative and positive lies our ancestors used, and that we still use to date. Probably no human has presented the contents and topics the book contains. If it happened that a book contained them, it would be in the form of passing remarks that are different from my direct, remarkable style."

At that moment, one of my friends who was sitting in another room approached us while holding his favourite drink and throwing nuts in his mouth. "Listen, guys. I've heard everything you just said, so in order to cut this lengthy conversation short go straight to the details. What type of lying is it?"

And now we will continue from the last question I was asked, "What type of lying is it?"

There is consensus among the public that lying is one of the bad characteristics, and that it is utterly undesired and indicates the dishonesty of people and their bad manners. However, if you examine the incidents of your daily life you will find out that they contain a lot of lies, and nobody has ever avoided using positive lying to perhaps, escape punishment, avoid embarrassing situations, to obtain a particular thing or many other reasons that the book will present. Therefore, we can say that the lying we will discuss in this book is a natural skill almost all people use. It pops up automatically when situations require it through our subconscious mind.

Once while I was reading a book late at night, I came across a sentence that echoed something inside me. Whenever I skipped it, I returned to read it again. The sentence was, 'Create value'. People, in general, innovate or create value through innately positive things; they utilise natural resources and process them into beneficial tools. They make houses of stone, paper from wood, jewellery and luxury watches of gold and heavy machinery of steel.

What if the book is about making lying one of the positive lifestyles or about innovating a positive value from things that have always been innately negative? What if nobody has used these things in the way that they actually deserve? Lying actually is one of these things.

This kind of lying is not a revolutionary idea that counters the established laws; it simply originates from the active universal laws. Everything has its own branches, whether they are positive or negative, and we can take what presents possible benefits for us. As we are human beings who enjoy complete freedom in our ideas and actions, we can deal with all existing things using our free will. This is not limited to tangible things; the existence of some things does not necessitate being a physical object or observing them with the naked eye. We do not see our words when we utter them; this does not mean that they do not exist. The effect of our speech is often seen in its impact on our senses.

Lying cannot be viewed from one negative perspective, and not being able to see the positive aspect does not mean it does not exist. This positive aspect will unlock its doors when we wish to get to know it, and it would unveil for us its social, psychological and mental skills and much more. The realities will differ instantly once our explanation or perspective differ regarding them.

Positive lying is actually a blessing whose explanation is still incomplete. Many ideologies and other laws tried so hard to neglect and hide its true shape, that we were no longer able to see many of its beneficial aspects. No commercial, social, political or academic course can but utilise the skills that positive lying gives to that course. It will not be that clear, in a way that reveals the alliance of that course with positive lying, because it terrifies the whole world. We see it in alternative ways that take the shape of abiding by the public interest.

Everything in life has two sides. In each side, the contents that signify its distinctness interconnect together. It is one thing, but it is distinguished by having two different sides. Nobody is obliged to adhere to one over the other. I have enough knowledge to be aware of the different sides and when I attempt to make you a liar, and when I describe some people as liars, or some things and actions as positive lies, I am not referring to the conventional meaning of lying. I am actually referring to positive lying that has a good aspect, that enjoys a lot of benefits. People do not hate positive lying that does not harm them. Even the divine religions have not prohibited it. All you need to do is to have a positive mentality and abandon the negative one, that would mix positive lying with harmful lying that we already know very well.

Positive lying has stories, realities and laws. What we need to do is to contemplate its realities and stories and compare them with actual human experiences to draw lessons. Its laws should be studied to apply them to yourself and other people. These steps are organised in order to clarify positive lying and show its tangible benefits.

This book may contain some intriguing topics and ideas, and you will notice that while reading it. It was reorganised and redrafted many times, to give you the biggest amount of enjoyment and benefit. At the same time however, I advise you to take it seriously because the topic might seem ordinary; nonetheless, it will be no more than ordinary if you are not aware of its correct understanding and application.

An Introduction to Positive Lying

'When you lie to yourself that you are going to obtain something, you will actually obtain it. When you lie to yourself that you are doing something, you will accomplish it. When you lie to yourself that you live in some place, you will find yourself in it. Reality is too limited to be sufficient for what we need.'

'One of the positive lying facts.'

One form of mental power controls a great portion of human resources and their validity. It controls the sensory aspects that make us aware of their existence. At some level, we have felt waves of the subconscious taking control over many tracks of our course of thoughts and different practices, and our consciousness was almost banned from the full control process. Intuition replaced the position of consciousness and repressed its agitation and urges. The logical direction of this process lies in seeking the aid of these natural forces that can be attracted, because taking hold of them is a logical matter within the reach of our abilities and conscious efforts.

We can utilise many images and various principles to underlie these powers to present them in the best possible style. These images can be limited and judgmental to some extent. Their effectivity depends on the possible impacts of each image on our emotions and mentalities. Balancing the expected advantages and disadvantages for each person and taking a side has nothing to do with the strength of the messages — or the images — and their principles.

If I am to sum up the meaning of positive lying in a few lines, I would say, 'It is the powers and mental shifts that you initiate in your internal conceptions, to change what things mean for you. It is a process similar to brainwashing yourself. It is also a neuro-linguistic programming process to develop your intellectual orientations and subsequently, to change your behaviour and please yourself at the same time. It will help us castrate fears and insecurities, invoke natural and universal powers whose existence we were not aware of and transform ordeals into real chances, so to make the thoughts that harbour our imaginations true.' We can do all of that through utilising some strategies that differ from the strategies we are used to utilising.

Positive lying is the second real world you live inside yourself. You influence it and it influences you. Its effects then have impacts on the real, external world. We can look at the matter as a game we play; the times we need to reshape the previously existing mental connections and renew them in a way that would yield positive results for us. It means changing our static, mental views which would result in dramatically changing our behaviour.

When you lie, you are assuming a broad level of mental flexibility and innate intelligence to give yourself at the end mental, unexpected, subconscious powers that start in the conscious level and rests in the subconscious level. Your abilities to create an internal world full of enthusiasm and energy would make you a person who no limit would be able to stop. In many instances, honesty causes boredom and weariness, that make us helpless in many situations.

The point is the mental resistance that makes your ideas shinier and bolder. Lying will provide your mind and body with feelings and tendencies that do not exist in the first place. Therefore, through lying we will create positive variables that suit our intellectual and psychological level. These innate tendencies will generate ideas that would surface and materialise in real forms, while previously they seemed illusory.

The positive lying tool can be used in two ways — direct and indirect.

The indirect way: This method relies on the spiritual motives to formulate images and beliefs that exceed our consciousness or ability to explain them. We notice that when we accomplish or obtain something, while other people failed to do it. If we had been aware of the risks and possible complexities, we would not have dared to take the first step.

The direct way: In this method, we rely on previously developed rules and standards. The bold, intentional advancement and challenging of concepts in this method is a clear, constant strategy. We are simultaneously practicing indirect lying. This time however, we are intentionally doing that well aware of the complexities that we may encounter. We are invoking natural powers and pushes of enthusiasm that our regular mentalities were unable to invoke.

Direct lying is the basis of this innovative process, whereas indirect lying is the subconscious taking hold over our mental abilities. Clever discrediting of anything is a process of denial to replace primitive human values with newer and more beneficial values.

Intentional lying	→	Direct lying
Unintentional lying	→	Indirect lying
Questioning sayings, cultures, events…	→	Smart discrediting

Positive lying does not rely on constant guidelines; it is based instead on mental flexibility that originates from the main centre of communicating our senses and thoughts. This lying might be one of the irregular and odd phenomena concerning some social and innovative aspects that actually, increase its innovative strategy. It leads to new ideas and results that occupy the first rank in the innovative process. Sooner or later, their expected effect goes beyond the limits of the idea itself.

'Never trust the limits of your current power; when you always act as if you are the strongest, you become the strongest.'
'One of the positive lying laws.'

This extension grants unfamiliar results that exceed the expectations. Rather than relying on the laws of attraction, positive thinking or the like, positive lying actually depends primarily on the intelligent control of the mind to organise its ideas and reprogram its thought systems — that are not fully developed in terms of their explanation or whose objectives are not clear — that are incompatible with the unique nature of each person. This control is eventually what will define the drives and their repercussions. The issue is as follows: everything we obtain in our lives does not exceed in most cases, the boundaries we assigned at the beginning. We, ourselves, established the foundations that will bear what we need to establish; consequently, we will not obtain more than what we planned initially. However, once we do not accept or believe in the barriers we created and lie about our abilities to go beyond these barriers, we will be ready to create a new expansion project, so we obtain more than what we expected because of the continuous process of ideas expansion.

We can alter our ideas and emotions to such a big extent that they can be non-objective. However, this objectivity will be proportional to the amount of benefits it yields for us. In light of the mind's ability to formulate images different from the expected ones and its ability to reshape them, we will always be able to meddle in its contents to live moments of unlimited innovation, power and tranquillity. It is a matter of choice; we reshape our mentalities and lifestyles in a direct, bold manner to make them more rational and beneficial, or we keep them in their deformed shapes that will eventually hinder us.

We may encounter times like those in which we endeavour to remember things we forgot like a name or features of a person, or information we read a while ago. At those moments, we see quick flashes about what we need to remember, but these attempts are similar to trying to catch words flashing before our eyes to read them. At the end, however, what makes us remember the things we forgot? Things like hearing a word that sounds like the forgotten piece of information and seeing a photo similar to the lost one shall make us recall the information and images for which we were looking. At that moment, our consciousness retrieves many things, and we start organising them anew, to extract all information related to the image or bit of information for which we are looking. This is the necessary clue to recall the whole matter.

When we feel that we are drifting from ourselves and perplexed concerning obtaining the best form of life, an encouraging word, a moving image, or a touching situation will awaken us. We will regain our consciousness to see ourselves clearly, and it will distance us from our unstable life. Nonetheless, we do not simultaneously guarantee obtaining what will awaken us to see our world and ourselves from a broader perspective. The best decision we can take is acting as if we possess or will possess, all necessary images and information that would grant us a stable, clearer life, and after that give our best effort to preserve this life.

Positive lying consequently, will not bound you to your present time. Emotions, events or people cannot stop you from living the conditions and broad expectations you harbour in your imagination and real self. This is substantiated by the deep mental spaces through which you will feel the cells of your brain becoming active, to ensure the reality of your thoughts. The mind has an ability to imagine the occurrence of non-existing things in the first place. In this way, we create innovative images that were not previously familiar.

We mean here that when you lie, you are embarking upon your work, well aware of its context. The boldness that will accompany you will be far greater than your limited rationality. Confusion and doubt within the context of work are signs of failure or inability that will happen soon. Lying will enable you to accomplish things no matter how complicated they are, through ignoring their difficulties or magnitudes as well as living your life in unconventional and comfortable ways at the same time. The lying tool will work on erasing the mental barriers that you may encounter or may prevail over you in different aspects of your life. You endeavour to convince yourself that you possess all the abilities you may need — even if you do not — when you face anything, and that you are intelligent enough to guarantee being able to move from the start to the end.

'Do not believe your current IQ; if you need to be smarter, act as if you are smarter.'
'One of the positive lying laws.'

Many people believe that lying is a bad tool or habit. They intentionally explain the word 'liar' as a person who is the furthest from credibility. However, this explanation has become obsolete nowadays and far away from the meaning we intend here. The explanation of 'lying' might be different, once its objective and way of employment are different. The same is true regarding any other thing in life. For example, you can use fire to set fire to yourself and other people or use it to warm yourself up, produce goods, cook food and for many other benefits. You can also use stones to build a house or a staircase to go up or to smash your skull and harm other people. You can use a knife to cut yourself or use it to satisfy many of your needs.

When we intend to perceive something in a subconscious way, we will not care for what will come in the future. The similarity might be in the problems centralised in a place near us, while we are unaware of them; therefore, they do not affect our emotions or confuse our thinking. Contrary to what we hear or see, when we are afraid of confusion we go back once again inside our safety shells. This perception represents a change in the course and laws of the game, but it may eventually cause difficulties to us because of misunderstandings and poor planning. If we do high quality planning in our minds and ignore the possible difficulties, we will have blocked the gap of tensions and negative future anticipations; you see the image first, and later start on drawing up its outline disregarding the passing sceptical thoughts.

By using the positive lying tool, you will deal with your external world rationally and with your inner world with your innate instinct and the emotions of creativity and peace. This will make our internal perceptions have tangible external impacts. We have a great ability to control our internal and external worlds. We stand in the middle at the borderline, so we often become confused about taking the path that attracts our emotions more. We enter at times and exit at others. All of this happens mostly in a fragmented way because we do not have a disciplined, organised mindset that enables us to control our emotions and ideas in the perfect way.

Each person has their internal world where they like to sneak every now and then. Only few people understand the reality of bringing it to their surroundings. You can see most minds drifting in their internal worlds of accomplishments and happiness; once their attention is drawn to the external world, their smile fades and signs of dissatisfaction prevail again.

'God likes lying that entails public benefits, and He detests honesty that aims for bad objectives.'
'One of the positive lying facts.'

Based on your inner innovations, you will be able to take hold of everything in the external environment. You will then begin to realise that what was fake from the inside appears a reality from the outside. Mastering the laws of positive lying will increase the depth of your inner perceptions so that you have the ability to see them as if they were in front of you. Your eyes might be at times wide open, but the depth of your distraction and preoccupation with your fantasies have taken you to the stage of seeing with the eye of the mind, so the seeing is extinguished from the outside and lit from the inside. This indicates that the mind is essentially free and moving to the place and time we want, trying to touch what matters to us more and feeling it will be far from disbelieving it.

What we have here is conclusive evidence of the ability to identify illusory concepts that seem to be real. Instead, you have the chance to prove your ability to attract hidden potentials that are more realistic than the ones on the surface. This change will be a liberation from the constraints, concepts and senses that we are accustomed to have within us. Consequently, this will increase our awareness of our ability to bring about significant changes in our material and spiritual worlds. This requires a special kind of perception that would shape our images and affect both what is visible and invisible in our world.

We humans are more than physical beings found at a certain time and place. Our ability to move spiritually and physically is much bigger than we think. By changing the concepts that monopolise our intellectual orientations, everything we understand and are aware of will completely transform in meaning. This relies mainly on the mental stimuli resulting from replacing scientific concepts. In fact, you are not locked up in the body you own now, and the whole universe revolves around you. This means that you have a considerable range of control and choice that you can yield to suit your ambitions. It is not possible to change clearly visible cosmic facts, but you can influence the psychological parts on the inside. Then, you will clearly see the great difference we can make in the outside world by controlling our inner world.

Every creature has a different perception with which they see the world, so they live in a world that varies from the one we know. For example, most animals do not know what depression or poverty mean, and their lives depend on lifestyles with practices that are completely different from that of humans. So they live lives that seem poor and painful to us, but for them they do not feel such things. Sea fish for example perceive the world, in all forms of life it contains, as a huge pool of salty water with some other additions that do not trespass the limits of the world that they are aware of. As for freshwater fish, they have a contrary perception as they do not even recognise salty water. The whole universe for them is nothing more than a running river. As for other creatures, the world for each species falls within the limits of its own perceptions. They see the world based on their nature rather than on the reality of the universe itself.

Similarly, our lives are dependent on false perceptions that we live without. Losing them would mean losing many aspects of our typical lives. For instance, if we throw a large sum of money in a crowded neighbourhood, it will vanish in a short time. What an individual perceives, is of great importance to him and to his environment. On the other hand, if we throw the same amount of money (or even a much larger sum) in a forest inhabited by many different creatures, we will find that it will remain untouched for quite a long time. In the world of animals, money does not have any value because the way of life does not depend on it. Ignoring the money does not reflect its non-existence, but rather not recognising its existence.

Having intellectual abilities and intelligence does not make men capable of perceiving the world for what it really is. Every human being sees the world according to his way of thinking and his personal concepts. You will see the universe based on your nature or inherent instinct. This explains the fact that some people go through the same living conditions and possibilities but show different reactions. The only difference is the flexibility or rigidity of their perceptions and their diverse personal concepts. Although human beings are different, they share many similar traits. These traits are mostly biological and only marginally psychological. This means that their bodies operate within a known biochemical system, but their psychological vitality and psychological control of all the body organs are different. This difference can have a great influence that would actually result in changes that would take us further away from the primitive interpretations of how the body and mind work together.

'Continue lying to yourself until your sight goes blind.'
'One of the positive lying laws.'

This is actually a process of manipulation and replacement of existence, a mental movement that is smarter than we can imagine because it is flexible, variable and renewable, giving us ideas and other ways that were not within the limits of our understanding or within our reality. Manipulation here is achieved by changing our distorted beliefs. As for the process of replacement, it is a step towards new discovery that would bring about the desired positive change. If we examine what is going on here, we will find that it is the same message that we are trying to reach: direct lying, intelligent discrediting and then changing what our world means to us with all its positive and negative events.

There is something greater that brings us into the universe; a deep spiritual intelligence that has vast limits and potentials. To understand it we need science, concentration and meditation, so we could get the right concepts or systems of thought required to understand our ability to spiritual mobility. Once we apply this method of thinking, artificial laws and ideas or any other restrictions will not have the ability to affect us. We are not affected by them because we are completely separated from them, even though our attachment to them seems clear. This attachment does not mean we agree or disagree with them; it simply means we are going along with them.

Positive lying is giving yourself the greatest authority because it is the greatest intellectual power. It is an effective motivational tool that can change your convictions about something you used to think that you could not obtain, into something you are capable of doing. That is, benefiting all people. It also means achieving goals initially inside yourself and then in reality. When you are imagining, you are occupying a place within the laws of positive lying because most probably, none of your imaginations have taken place yet. Once you indifferently lie to yourself that you possess all the things you think about, all the obstacles that were formed in your brain will fade away; lying has simplified them and reduced their risks or future difficulties.

Even if you do not know how much effort you need to exert and you do not have references to support you, lying to yourself that things will be simpler than expected will comfort you a lot. It will give you the first push of enthusiasm and passion. Through lying you can wake up forgetting that you need to sleep in the first place or wake up as if you have not slept for months. You will be able to make time pass at the speed of light or like a lame tortoise.

A lot of people utilised the lying tool in a direct way, and some others used it indirectly. What matters, however, is the results of using either the direct or the indirect lying. In light of the available examples that reflect reality and bring together people who used the lying tool in both ways, we will discover how they managed to get what no one expected, not even themselves perhaps.

Some people may think that it is a strange and somehow confusing way when a person lies to themselves to unleash their potentials and get rid of their fears, but if we think about that expression in depth, we will find it one of the strongest and best expressions ever. We often find ourselves unaware that we can do or get some things. Once you lie that you have everything you imagine and deny the existence of obstacles, you will be able to release the most courageous person in you; there is no fear of failure and no doubt about your ability to get the life you always imagined.

We are not here to always win; victory, however it comes to those who are courageous and brave, are self-aware and confidently believe in themselves. The truth is that positive lying may be greater than expressing it in ordinary words. It carries deep and mysterious fantasies, and the power of perceptions will vary from one person to another depending on their strong sense of imagination and the depth of these imaginations.

'Lying will carry you to worlds that will seem unreal at first sight, but sooner or later they will become real if you believe them.'
'One of the positive lying facts.'

Remember that when you become a liar, you will be that person you need in different situations. You will wear the right mask for every moment, position or person just like actors who become or turn into what they want and impress their fans with their pleasant and mysterious changes of characters. It does not mean that you have to forget yourself. Be always yourself until you see a need for a new mask that is suitable for the situation, and suitable to deal with some people. It is not bad to act when you deal with other people because it means that you have put your CV aside and started to adopt – temporarily — the rules of other people. In other words, you have started thinking as you like, but you treat people how they like.

Between Beneficial Lying and Destructive Honesty

'Lying will firstly take you to the real internal world that is full of enthusiasm and achievements. It will next take you to the real external world to reflect your thoughts there. Whereas destructive honesty shows you only the miserable facts in your internal and external worlds, and it keeps you adhering to them.'

'One of the positive lying facts.'

We often cannot analyse everything we see in the environment around us; we do what everyone else does, and we believe and follow the sayings, appearances and lifestyles of other people. The time we will need to look for new lifestyles that distinguish us, can be long and risky as well. Therefore, we follow and believe in everything that reached us from our parents and ancestors, and we eliminate the notion of discrediting the ideas and customs that control us and we do not analyse them to see whether they are compatible with us personally or with the present time.

Imagine that we put an infant in the hands of monkeys to bring the infant up. What would we expect the infant's environmental programming to be? The more the infant grows up, the more they look at their environment, believe it, learn from it and acquire the habits of its inhabitants, and the infant will live accordingly. It is true that the infant human will see their form somewhat differently from the surroundings, but it is not so important because all animals see themselves differently from others in certain degrees, including even those ones with the same animal family. As for us, the case is similar too because animals see us look alike in terms of our appearances and actions. That little human will not look at their truth but at the reality of the environment, the habits of the creatures around them and their lifestyles.

As humans it is true that we look alike, and we know our real biological families through nucleic acids or genetic instructions; we do not really know who our real environmental and educational families are. They are those people who are going to teach us the best ways of thinking and the purest beliefs and lifestyles when we meet them. We are similar in our appearances, but we are not alike in our lifestyles and mentalities. The lifestyles stand for our customs, and mentalities carry the personal values and principles. Since you will agree on the inability of monkeys to raise a human in accordance with the child's intellectual faculties, you will also agree on a person's inability to live without distinction. This distinction comes through discrediting what reached us from our ancestors, to be able to put aside outward appearances and study the internal, real value of what we see.

We live in an environment and look at it with what it carries for us without considering ourselves and our distinction. Eventually, it becomes a matter of luck. If I live in an environment that will offer me the best ways of life, I will be creative and distinguished. If the environment is bad, I will turn out to be bad. In both cases, I will not look at myself. I will only follow those people around me and believe everything that my eyes behold without discrediting their words or doubting their actions.

Never think that this analogy is that far from reality as you have imagined. What distinguishes humans from other creatures is only the ability to think and invent more creative and sophisticated ways of living. When someone abandons this advantage, that reign will collapse and distinguishing them will become difficult.

Eventually, we will be in the shoes of that infant if we do not discredit our environment and the sayings of people around us and lie to ourselves that we can fly away from wrong beliefs and the non-creative lifestyles. The issue is like a challenge. The side that will turn victorious inside you is either the destructive honesty or the positive lying.

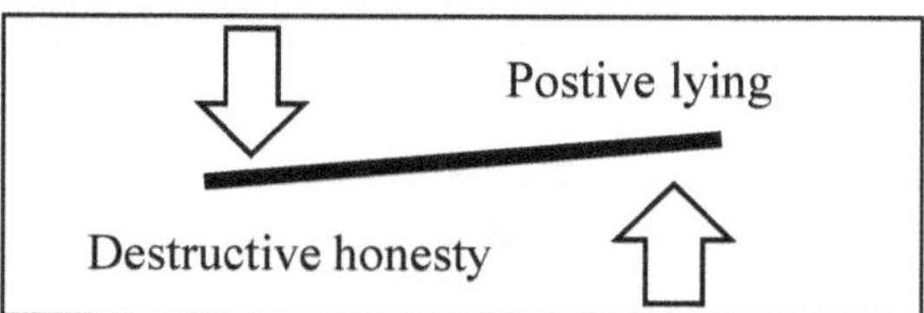

Positive lying represents the unconscious, while destructive honesty takes the place of the conscious. This conflict in our minds between the conscious and the unconscious will determine what we will obtain or achieve in our lives. We may need both the conscious and unconscious to carry out the various activities in our lives. The conscious, however, leads us to destructive honesty; it frustrates our movements because of the doubts and confusion it plants in our hearts. Positive lying on the other hand, is the foundation of the unconscious that proves everything we imagine and want to achieve. We finally feel that there are invisible forces that were helping us all along the way, without which we may have got into many troubles and wasted our efforts.

'A king wanted to know the fate of his wealth and whether it would suffice him for his whole life or if he would die after a struggle with poverty. He asked for answers from the best two soothsayers in the town. When they were summoned, the first said, "You will die bankrupt because of the large amount of your donations and your continued spending on your desires." The king was angry at this painful response and ordered the soothsayer be executed.

When the second soothsayer came, he said, "You will not die until you have helped your family and all the people of this town, as well as having fulfilled all your wishes and aspirations." The king rejoiced, thanked him and gave him a part of his wealth.'

One of the positive lying stories:

'When you change the expressions, the meaning changes, and actions subsequently change, too.'

No doubt that there are pros and cons of honesty in general as well as many damages that result from it. On the contrary, there are many advantages that a person can possess through practicing positive lying, and it cannot cause any trouble to the person at all unless it was misused. When honesty is misused, its concept will be different until it becomes what is called the 'destructive truth'. This kind of honesty makes the beholder unable to see anything except what they perceive with their eyes. In other words, the beholder will only see the reality of the few opportunities that dispel the power of their imagination, until their choice is to surrender to reality and believe it.

When we look at people who have ended up preoccupied with a life that has no meaning for them but boredom and remorse, it will be clear to us how honest they are. They were honest to themselves when they saw their reality controlling them and they believed it. They could not find perceptions better than those in front of their eyes, nor could they find the job they wanted to do. It was the reason why they fell in the pit of self-pity.

Some of the sayings that honest people always repeat:

'It will cost me a lot of money.'

'It will take me a lot of time to complete it.'

'What makes me guarantee the results?'

'This job will require considerable effort as well as potential difficulties.'

'I do not have any certificates; who will accept me?'

'I do not have the required scientific qualifications to accomplish this work.'

'I am pretty, but I wish I were a bit taller.'

'What my father says is true; I am like him!'

'It is not the same as before.'

'What will I earn from this?'

No doubt that everything above was indeed honest and referred to the truth; however, that honesty is the main cause of retreat. As Henry David Thoreau once said, 'Any fool can make a rule, and any fool will mind it.' An honest person believes in everything said by other people and follows their tracks. Such a person sees nothing beyond what their eyes perceive. The honest only see the reality and seek its approval. If the natural and environmental factors surrounding them do not encourage decision-making, they will stop immediately and then resort to redirecting their tracks. Honest people will do that each time they embark upon doing any business.

The language of destructive honesty:

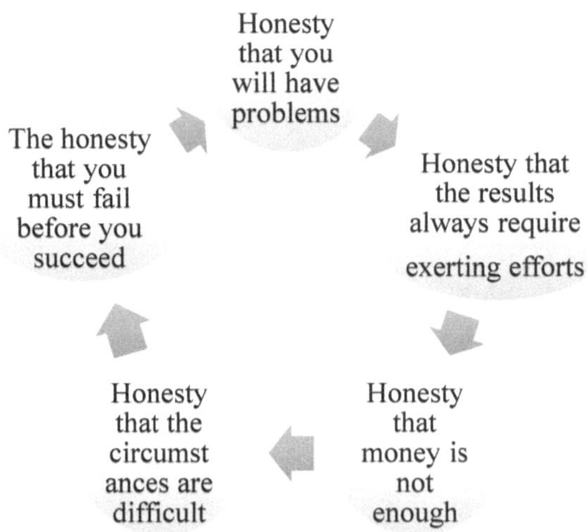

While looking at a person whom you find positive most of the time, you find them venturing to do anything without engaging themselves in a lot of complexities and explanations, in order to prevent fear of taking control over their mentality.

Negativity then, is to be honest to an ugly extent that makes us feel confused and dampens our enthusiasm and passion.

Some sayings of liars:

'I will never fail once I am certain of the context of an action.'

'It does not matter; I will finish soon, and everything needs time.'

'I do not acknowledge what is being said. I will try myself.'

'Things will change when one's perception is different.'

'There will not be bulky work when it is split into small parts.'

'There is nothing difficult. Difficulty is what one considers to be difficult.'

'I will guarantee the results regardless of the circumstances.'

'I will make a lot of money from that work.'

'I can learn a lot more than I know now. Life is much easier with learning.'

The previous statements or sentences may seem to be honest too, but most people use honesty in the negative form that we have shown earlier. Lying means that you lie to yourself positively even when the reality is completely contrary to your positivity. We may not be confident that we will reach results, while we will be able to simulate our imaginations to convey them to the real world. Consequently, we will have influenced these imaginations as well as being influenced by them.

If you take a thorough look at the content of the positive lying language and compare it to what the public say, you will find that it carries words and expressions that seem odd in a world full of many optimists. Therefore, these words and expressions will sound abnormal when we hear them repeated by one of the optimists. Positive lying does not mean carrying out any work without considering it and studying its consequences well; it actually means studying it and then planning it but with a mentality that is not afraid or doubtful about guaranteeing the result.

The language of positive lying:

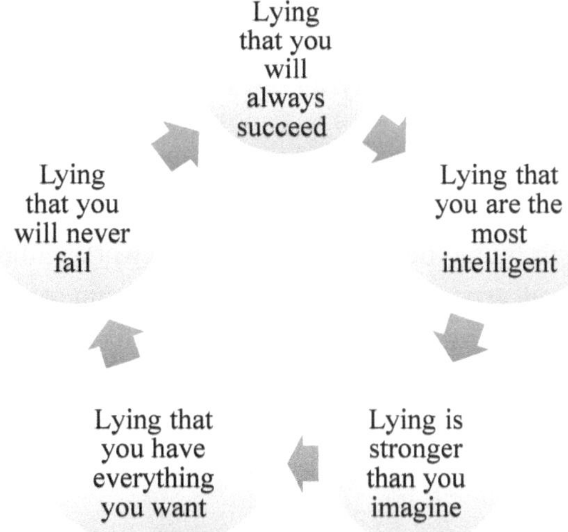

Words have a great impact on us. They are the content of our minds and lead us to a life whose quality depends on the words that we utter and say to ourselves. It may seem that repeating some sayings contradicts our present abilities and reality; however, the direct impact of our words will be clear and exciting enough to change ourselves and our perception of ourselves and our world, because words affect our nerves and activate our neurons; consequently, they will present us with new ideas constantly. Continuing to repeat positive statements, even if they do not seem realistic, means seeking more creative ideas as well as physical comfort and psychological relief. Our brains rely mainly on linguistic programming in formulating ideas and developing them, and eventually we will get the final programming that we have formulated with our words.

'Lie to yourself and pretend happiness, and you will not grieve for one day throughout your life.'
   'One of the positive lying laws.'

When you become a liar, you will be a different person who is able to make positive changes according to what you want to do. Through lying you can be resourceful, work without fear, increase your speed and gain a new domain of thinking differently from other people. You will be like children who always lie and say they are the smartest and the strongest. They also deny the bad conditions and the environment around them and do not recognise them. This is actually the secret of their happiness.

If some of the undesirable future situations were unveiled for us, we would perhaps wait helplessly for these events with tension and confusion until we overcome that stage. If we reverse this notion and unveil some of the future events that we desire and seek, we will spend our days looking forward with the most positive ways of thinking. We will in fact be exposed to those situations and events — the desirable and undesirable ones. Our sincere intellectual orientations will reveal to us those undesirable events, whereas positive lying only shows us what we hope for and wish to happen.

As we do not know what will happen to us, we do not feel any fear or tension. We will face many troubles in our lives and fix them with a big smile. This is what positive lying will do. If you do not think about the troubles that will happen to you, you will overcome mental preoccupation and nervous tension about the simple things that are beyond your control, because the thing that we do not know is something that does not exist. In our lives, we know that we will encounter a lot of troubles caused by some people or circumstances. Once we discredit them and lie to ourselves that they are trivial and not worth worrying about, they will become trivial and thinking about them will not be appealing. This is actually positive thinking in various forms and ways.

The shrewdest conmen in history have used lying to reach their objectives in the negative way. You will hear practiced the same method used by those clever conmen but in the positive way. We will put ourselves and others in the same position where the victim is looking for huge gains while in fact they will lose a lot. However, the difference will be that you will obtain those gains. Be a brilliant conman, not in robbing people, but in invoking their potential that they do not see. Cheat also on yourself to bring out treasures you never expected to have.

People often stop and wait for a long time before starting the work that they have always imagined. Some of them forget the existence of the whole process due to the long waiting period. They do not know in fact, that only a small push can get them out of the circle of confusion and fears. Fearing the results and risks of work undermines the readiness of personal efforts and delays doing the job until another time when their sense of security is firmer and clearer.

'Lie to yourself and act as if you will never fail; you will never fail. Be honest with yourself and act as if you will fail; you will fail.'
'One of the positive lying laws.'

We do not know how strong and intelligent we are except in few and rare times. Those times are either related to certain events or an urgent desire to invoke something of our inner self to the external world. Lying to oneself can be like living an illusion that helps us constantly extract natural powers that we would not have noticed previously. People always live in their dreams and inner thoughts. What makes them fearful is their frustrating mindset that makes them believe all the negative images that their environment presents them. This would make those creative ideas temporary. They become excited about a particular idea and sooner or later, their excitement fades when they discover the risks and required efforts to prove the existence of the idea.

You are here creating images inside your mind and living them safely with all your emotions. There is no confusion caused by possible obstacles and no significant worries about materialising these images, especially if the surrounding conditions are very difficult, because you will live most of them inside you. These images may seem illusions at the beginning. However, over the passage of time, our actions will indicate as if they were real.

Every human being can make their own future and sketch its outline, since there are some people among us who cannot change one of their ordeals such as a chronic illness that hinders them, or the political circumstances surrounding them. The mere attempt to internally develop anything and bring it to the external world will be dangerous or create difficulties. In such cases, the imaginations are more internal and emotional than concrete from the outside. Trying to translate some things to the external world may be like trying to recover your amputated hand. The lying tool will guide its owner to the inner peace of mind, if it is not available in the external world. Achieving things internally is sometimes similar to obtaining them and achieving them in the external world.

'The important thing about lying is not only the enthusiasm that it will introduce into your soul; rather, it's its speed in translating the ideas into tangible, real things.'
'One of the positive lying facts.'

In addition, entire populations need to use this effective tool. The Japanese people are the one that mastered it because they disproved all the frustration and pain they had during World War II. Honest communities however, always approve that they do not have sufficient resources, loyal local population, poor relations with other communities, and inadequate budget. Had the Japanese been true to themselves back then, they would not have made it onto the list of the most influential people among humankind.

If a liar is in a place, they will make it nicer, more comfortable and more enjoyable. You will find this person ignoring and disproving every bad thing among people and situations. They give you hope even if there is not any. On the other hand, people who practice destructive honesty are the most negative and realistic. The reality is always painful and serious, so people do not favour it at all and prefer imagination full of happiness and realising their dreams. Reality is often accompanied by pain, fatigue and injustice. Through positive lying we will have everything we want, not only internally, but soon after that, the impact of everything we believe in its existence inside us will be materialised in the external world.

The Most Common Uses of Positive Lying

'It seems that the time when people fight evil for the good is over, and we are at a time when we are fighting the worst for the bad.'

'One of the positive lying facts.'

The following are the most common and widespread forms of positive lying among people. They might be similar among them, but attitudes are still different. The forms of positive lying have been used throughout history, and almost all people still use them brilliantly up to date.

We have imposed upon ourselves many habits and things indirectly. The environment in which people live and the education they receive are what imposes the thinking styles on them. We imposed on ourselves using many of the behaviours and ideas we display in our daily lives, without even being aware of their existence. These forms of positive lying are some of those ideas and behaviours that we have introduced into our lives since our childhood, and we continue to rely on them in most situations we encounter.

Even those people we often hear saying, 'Lying is lying no matter what its forms are. It cannot have advantages or be used positively,' also use most forms of positive lying. If they are not aware of that, they use positive lying unintentionally. No one can evade the forms of positive lying that we are going to discuss because we have imposed upon ourselves using these forms. Ceasing to use them is an impossible matter, and there is no need for it because they all offer us great benefits, and this is a matter that you will be certain of very soon.

These forms of positive lying are an emotional and social skill. Being negative or positive is a matter that depends on how lying is used. The explanation presented below is meant to clarify its truth and its causes. It is also meant to show us how to use it in an ideal and positive manner.

Form one of positive lying: **When fighting wars.**

The most powerful weapon in the world, that was used in the past and is used these days, is not the sword, nor is it the nuclear bomb; it is actually deception and lying in wars. We have seen many victories in our region that logic cannot prove. In wars, the number of soldiers is not the determining factor of force, nor is it the number of weapons despite their importance. The real power is actually the power of reason in deceiving and lying.

One of the most famous and greatest lies of war in history is the 'Trojan Horse'. The beautiful horse that was more than one hundred metres long and was given as a gift to the Trojans, did not signify peace or lifting of the siege as it apparently looked. Had the Greek besieged the city of Troy for ten years, it would not have worked. However, coming up with a military positive lie of a large horse full of soldiers would not take much time and effort, to achieve a goal that failed to be met for ten years, succeed in a few hours.

All wars in history utilised the power of lying. Without this power, most great victories documented in history would not have happened. Even the strength of the most powerful countries in the world in the present time is measured not only by their weapons, but also in terms of the power of their deception. When a country wants to invade another country, it does not use nuclear bombs or deploy its army. Sometimes it does not have to send a single soldier. It uses the force of lying to collect information and make the enemy fight itself without getting involved in the process. In war, the greatest advantage is not possessing lethal weapons, as there is no point in having a lethal weapon without strong lies to support that weapon.

The Carthaginian commander, Hannibal, and his army made a terrible mistake during the Second Punic War when they were led into a closed area surrounded by the sea. When the Roman army knew that, they quickly besieged him and blocked all the passages. The situation for Hannibal and his army was like a slow death. By midnight, in order to survive this fatal situation, Hannibal used hundreds of bulls that he had been using to drag and carry the equipment of his army, as a trick to indicate the arrival of a new army to reinforce *his* army. Hannibal made their terrifying sounds louder, tied a lot of tree branches to their horns, and then set fire to the branches to make the situation look really dangerous. It appeared for the Roman army then, that huge reinforcements were coming from an unexpected place. There were a lot of terrifying sounds without a clear explanation for what was happening because of the pitch black. When the guards became terrified, they had to flee and withdraw.

'In war, the great powers are represented in lying and deceit, while the other powers are nothing but supplements.'
'One of the positive lying facts.'

The lying tool in war is often stronger than the weapons used. There are many situations in which weapons fail to save you, while the lying tool can get you out of any trouble no matter how hard it is. When you find yourself in war-like situations with some people, you can use the same tools as well. If we examine history in search for the true meaning of power in wars, you will not find it physical or related to weapons even though they were important.

The real power is the power of the trick through which you can defeat your enemy without even moving a finger of yours. Had power been the physical strength, animals would have controlled the earth. Lying in the battles you fight will be a great advantage that guarantees victory for you. If your enemy has more powerful weapons than you do, the better your war tricks are, the more victories you will achieve.

Form two of positive lying: **When we want to mend our relationships with other people.**

Lying to mend relationships among different people yields cooperative solutions through which all parties are satisfied. You can remember those situations when there was a disagreement with your friends or a family member and how you reacted. We actually may lie about the magnitude of the problem that other people encountered to mitigate its impact on them.

The best people in resolving conflicts and problems, are those who know how to solve the problems and remove their effects by denying their existence and magnitude. When there is a dispute between two people, and we are honest with them concerning the damage that may result later or concerning some of the disasters that will afflict them soon, we will increase the difficulties of these problems and multiply them so that they will take place in the present and the future. Once we deny their presence and persuade the other party in a smart way to not pay attention to pettiness, even if the truth is contrary to our words and far away from the fake optimism we made up, the influence of optimism soon after reaches the minds and feelings of others.

'Social relationships are pending one little unfortunate incident to end or a nice positive lie to last forever.'
   'One of the positive lying facts.'

We tend to use lying in the same way when we want to avoid losing some people. We do not seek to deny the reality but to start generating new ideas that help us draw ourselves closer to them without harming them. In addition, it is likely that the relationships among people – couples, friends, family members and work colleagues – might wane but what mends them and strengthens them again is positive lying that generates new ideas, and enthusiasm that enhances their interconnections.

Mending relationships among people is a natural skill that we use to mitigate the social conflicts we face, and it is one of the wisest and simplest acts. We do not like to see two different parties having a disagreement, so we try to create happy images to pacify those conflicting circumstances.

As the reasons for most disagreements are not worthy of concern and some of them are not even worth mentioning, we understand the circumstances of other people. If the positive lying we are using with the other party is not working, complaints and being honest that things will get worse are not going to be helpful; they will infuse the spirit of frustration and helplessness. By discarding undesirable things, we are actually pushing them into the past and preparing ourselves for a more beneficial and rational future.

Form three of positive lying: **When the truth is revealed.**

It will not be surprising to say that even the prophets used this form of lying, in many of their sublime stands. Let's take Jesus Christ as an example. He was eating with a man sitting on the bed of a river. They had three loaves of bread with them. They ate two loaves and one remained. When Prophet Jesus went to drink water from the river, he returned and could not find the third loaf of bread. He asked the other man about it and he responded that he did not know. After several attempts to make him confess, the man continued to deny.

Prophet Jesus then used another method to convince the man and make him admit what he did; he made three piles of earth, and prayed God to turn them into gold. Once it happened, the man asked him, 'Who owns all these piles of gold?'

He said, 'The first is mine, and the second is yours. The third is for the person who took the third loaf.'

The response came fast, 'It was me who took it.' The aim was not to give the man those piles of gold but to get him to confess what he did in an attractive manner. If we put what happened in the correct order, we will find that it is nothing more than a clever trick to pull the truth that we want and make it come out easily from the mouths of those people whom we think to be the most discreet people.

When we want to find out a fact or obtain some information indirectly, we use the same method. It is a skill to get the information you want without making the other party know what you are doing. In this method, we avoid a lot of effort and save time that we would have wasted on lengthy debates. We often toil ourselves in endless efforts to persuade and argue with others without reaching any result, except for more stubbornness and the making of new problems.

The psychiatrist, Milten Eriksson, used to lure his patients in an ingenious way to reveal their real problems. He used to manoeuvre and mention things and topics that had nothing to do with the problem of the patient or even with medicine. His goal was to detect the root causes of the disease. The expressions and stories that he used to tell the patient were linked to their psychological and emotional state and its underlying causes. If someone was suffering from an insecurity, Eriksson would tell some stories of people or even animals that had the same problem, the experiences they underwent, their causes and how they have been treated. When the basic roots of the patient's problem would gradually surface, Eriksson treated the problem with precision and indirect creative methods.

The benefits of positive lying in such situations are very useful. Doctor Milton and many others who use the same method have assured us that in many cases the patient may not be sufficiently aware of themselves or their case; therefore, they cannot describe their real problem and its underlying causes. The method of soliciting the requested information is one of the most effective methods. It extracts the information from the mouths of the people with all the accuracy and clarity without their knowledge. This method completely contradicts asking the patients directly about this information. The other party doubts and then has to evade some questions. When you ask for the desired information in one whole, you do not receive it in a clear order, and it may get lost while it is presented to you in one bulk.

To obtain any bit of information you want, use the luring method to uncover that fact so that you do not give the other party a chance to forget or avoid your goal. Things that come quietly and in an orderly manner are always more influential and more concise, than the things that come in one go in that they will not be organised and clear. If you try to drink water from a strong waterfall you will hurt yourself, and you will not quench your thirst. However, if you try to drink from a slowly flowing water tap, you will drink as much as you need. Do not force the facts you want to come out in one go because you will lose a lot of them; listen to them patiently so that you take hold of them.

'Needed facts are inherently difficult to obtain. When I pretend not to be aware of them, they come to me fast.'
'One of the positive lying laws.'

Many clever secret service officers know how to get the information out of the accused and make them confess their criminal acts. They use brilliant methods to get information. To reach the truth, they start inventing some events and situations that are related to the same subject but in disguised, indirect language or ways. They later study the comments they extracted from the accused carefully. The style we rely on here is like making up small lies that pull what we want inside a closed circle and take hold of it.

We can also learn from spies. The most brilliant spies throughout history used this method to find out the information and facts they were seeking. They are the cleverest people in taking hold of the mind and extracting ideas from the minds of their victims. They are like that person who started a small fire to see who would jump in the water first. It is not bad to become a spy for your own good and for the interest of others, as the best doctors do in spying on the ideas of their patients to solve their social and psychological problems. The most powerful leaders of countries also spy on their people to solve their economic problems and fulfil their needs. In addition, the most skilled managers spy on their institutions and employees to get rid of mistakes, increase productivity and empower their members. The best parents also spy on their children to monitor their actions and adjust them to increase the knowledge, insight and good morals of the children.

The reality we seek is often hidden behind the complex barriers within the brains of people and obtaining it directly and clearly from them, will be difficult enough so that we give up. On the other hand, the indirect method will reduce the amount of effort and time wasted, and it gives us the truth we want with the least time and effort.

Form four of positive lying: **When we save ourselves from difficult situations and avoid losing.**

Prophet Muhammad also used positive lying as a means to trick in fighting wars in many different situations. While he was emigrating one day with one of his companions, one of their opponents got in their way and asked his companion, 'Who is the man with you?'

He responded, 'He is a man who guides me to follow the correct path'. Their opponent thought that the man was really doing it, and he let them go. The intention of the Prophet and his companion was positive when they lied to him in order to continue their journey safely. Had he known the truth, no good would have happened.

There is no harm to us when we lie in hostile situations, but there will inevitably be a lot of harm and damage if we are honest. Honesty with your enemies has no point except that it will hurt you and cause trouble for you, or perhaps be the cause of your downfall. In hostile, difficult situations, learn to hide the painful truth that there is no use of mentioning, and use more imaginative and attractive ways to save yourself. The moment you save yourself from any difficult situation by using lies and tricks, you will show yourself and others that you are greater than that painful and dominant situation.

General Zhuge Liang, during the Three Kingdoms war, heard that a hostile army of tens of thousands of fighters was approaching the small city, where he was with a small number of his forces. He used an ingenious technique to get out of this difficult situation and avoid the huge loss that was about to befall him, because most of his troops had been commissioned to do other tasks. When he noticed the advance of these huge numbers of fighters, he did not prepare to fight or call his army back to defend him. He actually summoned forces far stronger than the power of armies and weapons; he opened the gates of the city and sat in a high place near one of the gates calmly and confidently as if sending a message to his enemies signalling welcome. The army thought that he was waiting for this moment and had prepared well for it, because there is no point that a great leader like Liang would open the gates of a whole city and sit in front of his enemy without any soldiers or protection, unless he was thinking of being beheaded. It must be a very professionally prepared trick that would smash his enemies in an unexpected way. The opponent army had no choice but to withdraw and retreat because there was not enough time to have an explanation for what was happening.

General Liang used a mighty style to lie to his enemy and deceive it skilfully. Perhaps he would not have won even if all his troops had been there; and even if he had won, he would have lost a lot of his troops and inflicted destruction on many places in the town. With that powerful lie, he defeated his enemy without even using one of his soldiers.

No power will enable you to defeat tens of thousands of soldiers when you are on your own except for a creative positive lie. General Liang defeated tens of thousands of soldiers on his own without moving a single organ of his body except his eyes. When you face a difficult situation and want to avoid the loss it may cause to you, what you have to do is to make up a new positive lie that will make your opponent collapse and retreat, and you will be able to get what you want. There is nothing more brilliant than that; you avoid loss, make your enemy flee, and obtain your objective in the end.

'Do not waste your time in fighting caused by your lack of planning experience. Just avoid the idea of fighting and control the enemy using a clever positive lie without any conflicts.'

'One of the positive lying laws.'

If we want to emerge out of a certain situation, or get something, we just have to understand the nature of these situations or things and study them well. History has shown us that the right way out of sudden, unexpected situations that will hurt us and make us lose our possessions is not a matter of conflict and blind challenges. Victory will be for those who have creative ideas that are far from emotional responses. We are not used to sudden changes, nor do we like them. When they take place, we start to panic without understanding the nature of the situation. Our excessive emotional response is the cause for our inability to keep pace with the changes. Hitting yourself against the walls of a prison cell in an attempt to get out of it will make you a prisoner forever, while inventing a new lie that fools the one who imprisoned you, will set you free easily, as soon as possible. Remember each time to not move your body at all before you stir your thoughts and make them spin and flounder inside your mind, to give yourself the chance to find the most appropriate thing to do.

Form five of positive lying: **When we want to look better.**

Pretending and trying to look better have become too clear recently. It has also become a habit for too many people, and we rarely see anyone who does not try to have a better look that has a greater value. Appearances have become the most essential thing, and what is invisible has become worthless, even if it is really valuable. We do things that we do not want others to see, we show other things when we deal with people, and we just do not do those things as soon as we are out of sight.

It is nice to constantly try to appear as best as they can when they deal with other people, even if it is just pretending. This would give a better charisma and image and may help to continually improve our actions and behaviours. It is not logical to display our bad habits to other people on the grounds that we are honest, and we do not fake our actions. Even the brilliant stars who have succeeded in making us think they are flawless are good at this technique. In fact, when you try to show your best form to someone, whether through acting or a trick you invented, you will not hurt or underestimate that person. You will actually make him happy to have met you.

The truth may sometimes be distressing and undeniable. If you now use your memory to retrieve most of your attitudes when you meet people, you will find that it has rarely happened that you have been yourself, and it was for a few times with specific people. Furthermore, you were each time trying to improve acting as if you have a better, brighter appearance. We often use this form and try to look better with people who are new to us or whom we do not know well. We are not ourselves, nor do we use our habits with people who we met due to our circumstances. We behave as per the circumstances and coincidences that come our way in order to get out of them again successfully and get back to being ourselves. As with the people who are close to us, with who we live, the lifestyle of acting and hiding defects may work for a good time, but it will be difficult to go on, and we will go back to our normal states.

Trying to look better is not an act of deception or robbing; it is just manipulating the real appearance and making it look better without turning away from the real self. What kind of harm would affect us from someone who is trying to show us the best form of them? In trying to appear better, most people do not aim to harm others whatsoever. There are certainly specific types of acting and pretence whose purposes are negative so as to harm the other party. We are not, however, discussing that harm, and we do not seek to reach it because many relationships ended, after one party discovered that the other party was not behaving upon his true, hideous, real self that had surfaced recently. Instead, that party was faking high standards and ethics that no longer existed anymore.

When we continuously say things and do the opposite, we will become fools in the eyes of others, and we will not find anyone who trusts us or believes us. We do not believe a single word of many people because of their blatant manner in trying to hide their sense of inferiority. Trying to look better does not mean saying and doing things you do not believe in. Rather, it is an attempt to look as a person who has attractive qualities, who likes to recognise all things that bear interest for themselves and others and practice them, even if we do not always practice them. In fact, many people do that. In this case, you have shown to others the positive things that everyone has to do and hidden the foolish things that you allowed to take hold of you. As for applying them, it is up to you; your views of acting upon them are all yours.

In the early 1820s, a young woman named Mary Baker from the English county of Devon was fed up with being a useless servant in society, as well as with her transfers from one job to another. Although she was a servant whom nobody knew and had nothing remarkable to impress people with, she had a great ambition and looked for a high social status. She devised a plan that would lift her status up to look bright, at least among a small number of people.

What Mary did was that she wore a strange-looking costume, made some changes to her face and invented a new accent and language. Then she went to a county in England. When she arrived, a large number of people gathered. After spending a lot of time trying to understand her, they managed to understand that she was a princess named Caraboo, and she came from an island in the Pacific Ocean. She confirmed that she had been kidnapped by pirates and fortunately managed to escape and jumped from the ship she was on board. She swam until she reached dry, English land.

It then seemed that they were looking at a heroine rather than a helpless, poor girl whom they could not understand. Not only did they praise her; they also began painting her! Sooner or later, she became the de facto ruler.

After a while, her truth was discovered and the trick she invented was unravelled; however, the aura she made for herself is still alive to this day. People who have a great social status and seek to achieve their goals boldly, truly deserve respect. The majority of those who have managed to reach high social levels have used similar methods to reach their goals without harming anyone. People who use their destructive honesty to look at their poor social, physical and social status will not be able to reach any valuable results. It is true that attitudes may be difficult, but they must be ignored to discover how difficult they are for us, to look at ourselves and to invoke all our skills.

Trying to look better makes it more difficult for others to discover your weaknesses. This bears great importance and power to enjoy among people. Uncovering your weaknesses makes you weaker, and people may exploit that weak gap that you revealed for latent purposes and to control you the way they wish.

'Hiding your flaws to try to look in the best form is not evil; beautiful appearances are well planned and do not come from nothing. They attract attention and raise the status of people. Even the green nature that seems to us to have embodied its nondescript appearance from nowhere, follows planned strategies. What is not apparent does not exist.'

'One of the positive lying facts.'

The situation is also similar when we tell stories that have happened to us, or when people tell us stories that have happened to them recently. We avoid some of the things that have already happened to us and we ignore them, or we may add some events to look better. On the other hand, we may change our behaviour in some situations for different purposes. We often like to do it because we like to impress other people and for them to be surprised.

Drawing attention to yourself gives you strength, an enchanting appearance and a high position you did not expect to have. If you do not have something tempting, using this form will give you a very attracting look. It is painful to be a forgotten person who does not impress others and is never mentioned anywhere. What should not be forgotten is that in the end, we will look how we pretend to be.

Form six of positive lying: **When we hide our emotions.**

Reality is often unattractive and difficult to believe. Instead, people like fantasies that tickle their emotions and make them feel happy. If you try to express your feelings freely and fully, you will receive large rejection and many attacks. Expressing our views freely is considered insolent from the social perspective. This is one thing that we learned from an early time. If you try to remember those times when you expressed your feelings frankly and freely, you will notice that there is not any similar case. If there were any cases, they may have been in times of anger and during quarrels that ended your relationship with some people. For this reason, hiding our emotions has become a valuable social skill; people know well what they should say and what they should keep for themselves. We can see how people are always keen to select words before uttering them in someone's ear. Expressing our feelings has become an indicator of selfishness and a kind of losing of self-control.

The most talented and loved people among others are those who know well how to conceal their emotions and emit a shine, significantly because of the power of their minds. They apparently behave in a manner that suits the other side even if they disagree with them. On the other side, nonetheless, they may conceal contrary beliefs that they reveal only at appropriate times. The human nature has always proved that. People do not like those who do not recognise them, disdain their beliefs and underestimate their ideas even indirectly. Therefore, the matter of purchasing a mask for yourself is not immoral anymore. On the other hand, it is cheap, but its effects are priceless.

'Concealing emotions indicates the existence of the power of self-control that is one of the most important moral acts. The moment we lose the ability to control and hide our emotions, we will look like losing ourselves. This is what

distinguishes humans from other creatures the most; it is our ability to control our lusts and not run behind them. If humans lose this ability, they will lose their humanity.'

'One of the positive lying facts.'

Many people among us like to brag about their unusual and offensive ideas, and these ideas often hurt others because they are not qualified to hear what we say. Even if your ideas are creative and unfamiliar, they may appear to others in a way that you would not expect. When we address people, we must first consider their knowledge about the affair. For them at least, neglecting to consider their knowledge represents contempt for them and insults their pride and their modest nature. Be creative with your new and unusual thoughts, and humble towards the simple and familiar thoughts of other people. You will then look like someone who other people feel happy to meet.

Master the art of hiding your feelings as a kind of respect for the values and customs of others, to look as one of them; especially your feelings of sadness so that no one feels it. In the end, nobody will care about it; even the closest people to you, will not get from them that great benefit. We can learn to hide our feelings from animals; they do have feelings, but they rarely make you feel them. Life will not go well without using your skills that are remote from your feelings; understand your feelings and do not make them overwhelm you and impede you all the time.

Form seven of positive lying: **When we do not want to clarify expectations.**

The lack of clarifying expectations is a process of substituting potential events, i.e. events expected to happen.

We are here replacing a reality with another reality by making or inventing the means leading to it. This is a motivational strategy that brings the difficult goals closer and makes them more attainable. Increasing the probability of what we want to reach will increase the likelihood of it happening. Reversing the rules and exaggerating the negative expectations will only increase the spirit of frustration and fear in the soul.

We do not want to show the painful reality because it undermines the determination and generates frustration in our hearts. The safest thing is to refer to the positive expectations and predict their occurrence in the world of the unseen, as that is the foundation on which all the victories are created. The persistence in clarifying the expectations that show us facts about looming potential losses will inevitably give us undesirable counterproductive results. The stimulus is a process that exceeds the limits of the narrow logic that we have.

'There was a general who would take the news of the death of someone close to him easier than losing a war he was leading. Losing in his life was one of the greatest tribulations. What he did was that he summoned a soothsayer and convinced his soldiers that he was one of the smartest soothsayers of the times. In order to prove it as soon as possible, the general agreed with his soothsayer to make prophecies that certain things will happen at specific times, and then the general planned to make what the soothsayer predicted an actual reality. Not so long later, the words of the soothsayer became like magic to the soldiers because none of his prophecies ever failed to take place. He used to expect an explosion in an area or

someone's illness, and everything he said became true. However, in reality things were different. The general, his soothsayer and some of their aides planned everything. The aim of all this was the importance of what the soothsayer would say at times of war. When they got ready for the next war, the king summoned the soothsayer and told him in front of all his soldiers, 'Tell us what you have seen. Are we going to win or be defeated?'

Then the answer came as professionally as follows, 'If the issue is about victory, do not be afraid soldiers, it is yours today!' To make it as if it were an undeniable fact, he added, 'But Sir, there will be a weakness for the soldiers you have assigned to observe the eastern side of the battle. My advice is to add twenty soldiers to that side, so we will have saved ourselves excessive pressure on our soldiers and closed the gap.' Once the soldiers heard it from their soothsayer, who never happened to make wrong predictions, they marched to the battle with enthusiasm, as if they would never lose. Accordingly, by creating another comfortable reality and tampering with soldiers' fantasies, no war was lost.

One of the positive lying stories: People do not like the truth because it confuses them and gets them out of their true selves. Instead, create a reality that others enjoy delving into with their imaginations, so you increase their spiritual and mental powers and make a history to be remembered.

What happened was actually all we really needed, i.e. to act as if we would never lose but in a direct way. On the other hand, the indirect way will come to you to motivate you as it did to the soldiers, but you rarely get exposed to this method, and it is easier to master using it yourself. The general mastered using the indirect lying way to motivate his soldiers, and the soldiers lied to themselves by using the indirect method to motivate themselves, too. They would not have expected to fail after seeing the fabricated fact that they would never fail.

The analogy will be this example: how would you respond if you were offered an insect to eat? It may seem gruesome and eating that insect would be a psychological torment. But what if someone put that insect in one of your favourite meals? You may eat it easily, and perhaps even enjoy its delicious taste. This is what lying does in general. It hides those confusing images and replaces them with a safer one. The general did the same. If the soldiers were aware of the difficulty of the battles they were to fight, the victory would have been more difficult than expected.

Explaining expectations is a destructive honesty. Once you are honest in explaining things and what dwells in your imagination and the imagination of others, you will put yourself and others in difficult and embarrassing situations. No sharply intelligent person who knows how to control their feelings will unveil the reality of their actions and intentions easily, to make them clearly visible to all people. Abstaining from clarifying expectations is not just a way to hide feelings; rather, it is a kind of avoidance of a future loss that is likely to take place, if we persist in our excessive honesty towards people and their attitudes. In the end, it depends on our ultimate goal; if it is positive, either clarifying or concealing expectations serves us and other people, too.

Form eight of positive lying: **Compliments.**

We can consider compliments as one of the most common forms of positive lying. It is a habit that has been embraced by societies for ages, and only few people cannot master this form. It is useful and easy to use. Compliments are one of the most important codes that people depend on when they deal with each other. If you consider the truth of compliments, you will be sure that they are untrue statements and found only to show respect for the other side, to appear better, to not embarrass someone and many other reasons. People inherently have overwhelming emotions, and the simplest of words have a meaning and a big impact on them. Even those small words that come out of us unintentionally may mean a lot to others. The human nature confirms that to us as it cannot give up compliments. Otherwise, communication will suffer disruptions and troubles will increase among people.

People are sick of hearing the bitter truth and have stored in their hearts their suffice of pain caused to them by other people who were confusingly frank. You can see how when you deal with someone you do not really want to see; you will not be frank with them and tell them you hate them. You will actually compliment them to get rid of them. The moment you are honest with what you truly feel about others, you will have involved yourself in unnecessary troubles.

The English people criticised the French writer Voltaire who was living in exile. They wanted him dead because of the emotions he demonstrated against the French people for many reasons. He could do nothing but innovate a letter that bore a positive lie in the form of an attractive compliment. He published a speech to the angry people saying, 'Great people of the United Kingdom, do you want to kill me only because I am French? Do you not know that not being born an Englishman represents execution whilst I am alive? This is one of the biggest calamities that has ever happened in my life.' This was one of the strongest compliments the English people heard at the time, and he successfully saved himself so professionally from a certain death.

The entire nation was calling for the execution of the Frenchman whom they regarded as hostile to them; however, the compliment of Voltaire had extinguished the negative feelings towards the French. The truth was still there, but the compliment concealed it because people like to hear words that praise them and raise their status, even if they do not deserve what you actually say. You will not lose anything when you compliment and praise others. Rather, you will have a lot of victories and love.

'When you go along with the wishes of others and show your faith in what they believe in, not only do you cultivate the spirit of friendship and avoid long, provocative debates, you also spare yourself fierce attacks that you would encounter because of your strong adherence to what others do not believe in.'

'One of the positive lying laws.'

Form nine of positive lying: **When we want to get out of or save someone from an embarrassing situation.**

One of the most difficult situations a person may face is the moment of embarrassment. When someone is in an awkward situation, it means that they will take a defensive position as they start to feel abandoned and self-pity. Embarrassment is one of the most time-draining things to deal with and handle. To avoid embarrassment, we use our mental and emotional skills to get out of the situation. Our creative mind is often what provides us with this skill, and it brings out the best we can do, to avoid the embarrassment we have been exposed to. You must have remembered those times when you found yourself trapped in the middle of the sarcastic thoughts of others. What did you do? You may have made others look at you in a different way by an idea you invented or an action you did. Here you use your ability to evade events that put you in an awkward and difficult situation that damages your reputation.

Most of us have emotional intelligence. We pretend that we did not know, see, hear or understand something, were not present in a place at a specific time, not told of what happened or even pretend to have an emergency and make groundless excuses in addition to other methods, in which we seek to ensure that we do not put ourselves and others in an embarrassing situation. We also ignore errors to maintain friendliness or to stay in the safety zone to say the least. Emerging safe from an embarrassing situation is exactly like rescuing others in similar situations.

There are many bad actions people committed in the past that make them afraid of being exposed one day. What they do is create events, situations and ideas to make others forget them and keep themselves above suspicion. People are by nature afraid of abuse, and they do not forget it. Your skill in avoiding any abuse and departing from the past depends on your skill in denying those situations. If one person has a bad reputation for something in the past and wants to survey that incident, it is not impossible. However, it is often difficult to convince other people to forget that incident. To achieve it, that person has only to deny the past by linking themselves to a better past, or a more successful future.

In other words, some embarrassing situations are associated with the past such as reputation and associated with the present and the future and may often bring us some troubles. In order to be genius at overcoming these ordeals, we must do plastic surgery on these distorted situations, so it becomes difficult to distinguish them.

'A thief's guilty conscience for stealing people's money made him decide to return it. The problem was how to do it. Truth would bring him sharp attacks of revenge. What he did was that he went to some relatives of his victims under pseudonyms and asked them to return the debts because he was unable to reach the money owners due to unreal causes he invented. With another group, he claimed to have found some money near their houses and threw it their way as if it were nothing more than a coincidence, and many other similar ways. Through the positive lie, he doubled the gains — returned the money to the owners and distanced himself from any suspicions.'

One of the positive lying stories: Do not implicate yourself while thinking you are doing the right thing with your honesty. Get everything you want and get yourself out of any unwanted situation by indirect methods that bring justice to all parties.

If we look at the previous story, we see that when the young man decided to free himself from his embarrassing and scandalous past, he was sure that he would have destroyed himself had he followed the path of truth. Instead, he resorted to positive lying to please himself and his victims. If he had confessed his past actions, he would have quickly destroyed his reputation, ruined his life, and received attacks from all his victims before entering his new cell. However, the way he emerged out of the embarrassing situation saved him and preserved the rights of his victims. This is the best way to get out of such embarrassing situations.

People do the same thing; if we did bad things in the past that we want to correct, we will damage our reputation and put ourselves in unpleasing situations if we do not carefully put together a plan to get out of that dark past. We can borrow a positive lie that rids us of any predicament and returns to others their rights as well.

'Avoid the miserable positions, manipulate useless facts and hide their impacts. Consequently, you will overcome negative backgrounds that others will not have the power to forget, and you will create a creative, positive success that revives the heart again.'

'One of the positive lying laws.'

This kind of lying seeks to benefit all parties. The person who miraculously escaped from the gallows and went on to boast openly about it is likely to be hanged later. Do not expose yourself by your destructive honesty and by your outrageous and harmful feelings. Learn to avoid damage using ways and methods that satisfy all parties.

Form ten of positive lying: **Changing the subject.**

We often change the subject for one reason or another. Once we see that the conversation will take us to embarrassing topics, bring us back to painful memories, reveal a defect in us or uncover a secret we change the topic and purpose of the conversation indirectly and skilfully. If we do not apply this form on a daily basis, it will not be too long before we apply it from time to time for several reasons.

It is an ingenious way of escaping talking with another person, in addition to taking care not to embarrass others. Fortunately, most people will notice it when you change the subject, and they understand the reason, so they deliberately will not ask again or talk about what made you escape. Humans are creatures that have feelings, and they understand each other very quickly. Do not be afraid or embarrassed that someone will notice when you deliberately change the subject because they will understand your goal, and it does not have any kind of disrespect or embarrassment.

'Continue to change the course of discussions whenever there is a fair reason to do that, in order to let others know the importance of not engaging in long, provocative debates, and also not to interfere in what no one has the right to intervene in. Changing the course of questions addressed to us is an act of privacy for us. Not talking about topics that bother others is a great social and emotional skill.'

'One of the positive lying laws.'

Finally, changing the course of speech is a good way to express what you cannot express with words, and it is a sophisticated way to say words that are unwanted by the other party. Changing the topic will increase our social skills and create a pleasant and enjoyable atmosphere among all parties.

Direct Lying Dynamism

'There are mysterious, unintelligible but pleasant forces and we do not know where they reside. They come and go in the form of quick glimpses, and when our brains are full of vigour and enthusiasm. In fact, when we lie we attract and possess those big mental and physical forces and they will actually appear to us in forms we have never imagined. Only then our lives will not know the helplessness that is always bought by our thinking, which believes in its negative environment.'

'One of the positive lying laws.'

The information we directly and deliberately instil in our brains will be transformed into facts through the data conversion process, in order to translate them into things that require understanding. Our brain cells will communicate and spare every effort to store them and make them a reliable basis for the facts on which our conscious thinking is based. These parameters will eventually turn into facts and intellectual systems, based on which the mind works toward interacting with different events and situations, in the way it is trained.

This means that the normal communication created by the brain is not inherently established to take a specific approach as the thought that prevailed in the past and still occupies a position now. This hypothesis is not emphatically and fully studied. The brain has the flexibility to change itself and its intellectual orientations in a clear way. This requires certain situations and methods different from the rigid pattern. Direct lying provides the ability to transgress the usual stage of thinking and break the rigid stereotypes in us, with a view to increase our mental flexibility and change the classical learning strategy.

When you surpass useless learning methods, you will rise above your limited beliefs and move on to more creative stages. This transition will not be merely imaginary dimensions that we deliberately make, but it will quickly turn into concrete possibilities and thoughts. The brain is inherently obedient and will make every effort to transform the information that has been implanted within it, into actions that are consistent with its scientific content. In the later stages, development and building of information that is maintained in the brain will be initiated. A good thought usually comes up with a better and more appropriate development thought. Our role at this stage is to maintain this high level of continuous improvement by awakening the creative and constantly improving mind, developing new additions inspired by our thoughts and destroying useless, old beliefs.

I can interpret direct lying as follows: Our brains are full of intellectual rules. Our society, from members of the family and the educational environment, played a great role in finding them within us, and by the time we instil in our brains new, more bold and wise thoughts through our direct lying, we will automatically stone the artificial barriers that we formed unconsciously, toss useless beliefs and replace them with ways of thinking that conform to our creative potential.

The communication networks that the brain employs are numerous and can be easily increased at all times. The human mind is so obedient to the extent that we can change its content and intellectual connections very quickly. Thus, we can take advantage of these forces in order to transform oneself in all aspects. Signs of suspicion of possible conflict between our creative potentials and what we seek to invent and bring into existence are often unrealistic. These are just imaginary barriers our minds used to see, and they are the result of previous intellectual programming. This does not require a miracle; all those who have made achievements that inherently appear to be beyond human capacities, possessed a bold thinking that played a key role in moving beyond what is normal and presenting works that seem to be beyond normal human capacity.

Direct lying depends on two basic laws:

A. Persistence in trespassing the limits of natural potential. It seems clear that what is apparent or what we have reached is all that our natural abilities have enabled us to do and achieve. In such circumstances, we will believe that our ability to overcome these limits will be realistic only for those who possess a rare, natural intelligence and those are only a lucky few.

Persistence here lies in breaking the barrier that perhaps no one dares to defy or even think of. As we turn the pages of history, we find that the numbers that were standard one day became normal numbers today. They are even despised and are not recognised. The reason for this lies in the emergence of that person who trespassed in order to land the first place. Persisting to surpass this stage is to no avail.

In fact, there is no limit to persistence, even if it indicates unrealistic beliefs. Indeed, we find some thoughts that had previously been mocked, cross the bounds of reality and impose themselves. Even those who used to accuse these thoughts for being imprudent will follow the public benefits they entail.

The persistence that we see happening and that we want to create is not an immoral process that transcends the rights of other systems. It is a moral persistence that breaks through the current stages boldly in an uncommon way. We are not forced to lock ourselves at a certain stage with regard to all aspects of creative life. Our attempts to look for improvements must be continuous and uninterrupted.

There are time limitations to accomplishing any task, no matter how small it is. Nothing comes or occurs in a moment or at once, and that's what most people agree on. However, most of the changes we see did not require much time to occur. They happen at a glance because one gets to a point where he is mindful of the more precise strategies that would turn things around. This will eventually enable him to discover the reason why he has not achieved his goal in the past years, when he was trying through trial and error.

Thus, what we see and will see happening will not be just the result of coincidence or luck, but a moment of insight and thought which one summed up his whole life. In order to possess one of those moments of insight, we must deliberately and directly attract them. Chance will have no role in that. Direct lying is the complete control over our natural instincts and intellectual desires. Through direct lying we will attract the moments that will make us aware of what we do and what is really happening to us. Only then can we take the appropriate decision in order to resolve matters as fast and as conveniently as possible.

Our feeling that we are alive is not enough; the fact that we see, hear and feel does not indicate that we are living. The clear and only evidence that we are truly living lies in the fact that we are aware of who we are; that is to say, the precise knowledge of ourselves. This task may not be that easy. Deep, self-knowledge requires a broad and comprehensive knowledge of our human nature and the components of our universe. Judging from this step, we will walk armed with enough knowledge, to deal with all direct and indirect incidents with an aim to eliminate or add whatever we want in our lives. Through direct lying, and with persistence in particular, we will not only seek to know more about ourselves, but we will also constantly nourish them with forces that make us truly distinct from others.

When Edmund Hillary and his companions attempted to climb Mount Everest for the first time, their attempt was fruitless; besides, some of his colleagues died because of the risks they encountered. A press conference was held upon his return. During the conference, a photo of Mount Everest appeared behind him. He immediately stood in front of it and said, waving his fist, 'You're really huge, but I'll always be bigger.'

The direct lie was clear here; how can a man be bigger than a mountain that is about nine thousand metres high? These moments of persistence are not what we see or hear; they seem unreal at first. Yet, when Edmund said to the mountain, 'I'm bigger than you,' he really became bigger. You cannot see that from the outside, but you will definitely see a size that matches the size of that mountain when you have a look at what is inside of him. Edmund knew that he did not succeed in climbing it the first time, and that his abilities were not fully exploited, or perhaps did not allow him to do so. At that moment, he surpassed himself as being bigger than Mount Everest; and he was able to instil in himself beliefs beyond the real and common stereotype.

The matter is not just about the accumulation of information, rather about the quality and organisation of information. Once we desire to guide ourselves through a direct lie, we should adhere to the rules of the game. Every goal has a strategy and a thought that makes its huge size smaller and its difficulty easier. Nothing can be achieved through a messy inaccurate approach. Rather, every direct lie is followed by precise planning that combines and organises forms of knowledge to help us overcome potential mines in our ways.

The lying tool is not a mere powerful mental perception; rather it is an effective tool that forces its user to utilise all their potential, directly or indirectly. It shows us images beyond reality, the forms of which are not familiar or usual. That's what makes it occupy a prominent place in terms of human powers.

George Dantzg is a clear example. When he was still a student at university, he showed up late for one of his lectures. He found that his teacher had written two mathematical problems on the board. He jotted down these two problems thinking they were homework for him and his friends to do at home. He handed over the solutions a few days later, saying he had some difficulties in solving them, but he did it anyway and apologised for the delay.

A few weeks later, George discovered that the two problems that he solved were two mathematical dilemmas; no one had been able to solve them before. That was why they were presented in the lecture.

Let us go back to the time before George could solve these problems, and imagine the following: his teacher's request, simply, to decipher these codes because they are two mathematical dilemmas and no one has been able to find a solution for them and most importantly, to do that in just a few days. George will think this is one of the nicest jokes he has ever heard in his life. He now knows the potential risks and would not dare to work on them.

Had he been present that day, he would have resorted to the destructive truth and could not have solved them. Even if he had known the truth of those problems and resorted to direct lying to himself, he would have imagined the strength of the situation he experienced at the first attempt (while using indirect lying) and he would have got rid of the difficult and realistic beliefs that would have attacked him. He relied on indirect lying when he started solving these problems because he did not think of any possibilities for failure or of its consequences. He denied the difficulty of solving the two problems indirectly and was ready to confront them.

The issue resembles folding inferior ideas that are imposed upon us as we walk our way in life. Lying will give us the opportunity to look at the reality of things and erase past beliefs that convinced us that we are not qualified. If we were faced with a similar situation and we knew the difficulty we may face, using direct lying and bold persistence on events would enable us to change the whole experience. George was sending orders to his mind with confidence and transparency, that convinced him that there was nothing to make just two problems difficult, and they must be part of a regular university lesson presented to everyone.

'In a few seconds, you can hate anything you love and love what you hate. You can make what is hard easy or make what is easy extremely difficult.'
'One of the positive lying facts.'

Some may think that direct lying depends primarily on virtual existence. Getting the thoughts we create inside us out, to find them in our reality may not be guaranteed, or even logical. Yet, this is not accurate. The virtual world is the creator of the real world, and every thought that has improved our lives was once residing in the virtual existence before it appeared. There is no book or catalogue that illustrates the developmental process that we must follow, and the credit of these improved transitions is what we boldly invented in our imaginations and brought to concrete reality.

In view of that, there are two kinds of false assumptions: applicable assumptions and those beyond human capacity. Judging the achievable hypothesis out of others that are beyond our natural capacity will not be easy. The most guaranteed course for us is to study the nature of what we want to own. Most of the thoughts that already exist were not far from human capacity or were even unbelievable, but the wisdom lay in the author's careful study and deep sense of what he imagined. He is the main cause of its existence.

Following common sense may not be logical in itself; accordingly, how can we bind ourselves to a boundless reality when we witness new changes every day? It is illogical to set imaginary boundaries for an area with indefinite extent. At the same time, logic is full of terrible and frustrating facts. It also lacks creative imaginations that would create a better reality. Therefore, it is illogical to follow logic all the time. This will only push us back; additionally, taking things too seriously would only make small things annoyingly big.

Indeed, we may have gone extra miles with these measures, but we are referring to the stages of positive lying. It is not a complex process that forces us to exert our power in things we are unsure we can get. In a matter of minutes or seconds, we can see and feel that we own all that we imagine. Advanced steps lie in doing our best to make the outside world see what we already have within us. This is a complementary process; the beginning is from the inside and soon we are tempted to help it extend outward.

At this point, we persist in achieving what we imagine to the extreme, even those thoughts that seem too far from our abilities to imagine. We see how, when our enthusiasm is high and our brains are totally clear, we are prepared to exert the maximum effort and to not recognise the delusive barriers in order to reach a certain point. This transition point is all that we need even if it is temporary. As you remember, it is more like a game to play with in the places and at the time we want.

Each thought has its own roots, and these roots did not come out of nowhere; someone was involved in planting them. Instead of distracting ourselves by looking for those who planted them, it would be better to evaluate the information that we maintain and rely on in our lives, and then look at the available alternatives for development, if needed.

Direct lying is the process of planting new thoughts that are more compatible with our original goals and personalities. With our new thoughts, we change our present lives and create another in which our souls, bodies and minds are at their highest level of activity and filled with satisfaction and reassurance. Therefore, the intentional destruction of the former ways of thinking is the first step towards the bold progression headed for acquiring new information. Nothing will make us change ourselves and plant new systems through which we live except, our reasonable thinking.

We have often heard people (teachers, family and friends) telling us during school days as we prepare for exams, 'Do not set limits to the degrees you want to obtain, but try hard to convince yourself that you want to get higher than you expect.' When we try to comprehend the actual truth of the matter, it will become clear that they are using one of the guiding principles of positive lying, which is based on constantly growing new thoughts. This would be apparent if someone went to take a test that he had studied well for but set artificial limits for what he wanted to reach. On the other hand, which may seem difficult and unrealistic, giving answers to questions we have not studied before would be realistic if we used direct lying and supplied our brains with orders that force them to do something.

'For many years, the bird kept on rubbing its tiny blunt beak in the cage wire because of its boredom of living a restricted unfree life, but its efforts went down the drain. Consequently, it pretended to be dead, and when his owner took it out to check on it, he discovered what the bird had planned; he saw it flying away into that sky of freedom.'

One of the positive lying stories: Do not follow the usual difficult and miserable paths, a small direct lie may grant you a free life.

We can study all social, practical and psychological systems to instil appropriate thoughts. Each system needs certain rules to be practiced in a way that suits us and to be dealt with in the best possible manner. Before embarking on such a step, the roots of contaminated thoughts must be rooted out to make sure nothing will infect or hinder our new thinking methods. A bad thought we hold may eliminate many of our valuable thoughts.

Direct lying is both a regulatory and developmental process of thought and life systems, especially those we did not have any stake in. Even those thoughts that seem to be valuable and that strive for the benefit of all, will have a different effect from one person to another. Some of us will take them seriously and reliably in his life, and others will not feel the positive effects they possess. In the long run, this arrangement will give us a great deal of control, and that would protect us from slipping upon any collisions with other opinions.

Therefore, one of the false moves is to live life by methods of fighting. Victories come only to those who wait a long time and take enough time before taking any step. Our life is like a game of chess; it is a war. We cannot win without a clever mindset that relies on patience in taking every step, and that studies it well before embarking on it. The mentality that lacks planning does not know what to do and what fate it will encounter. It will fall prey to any hunter.

Direct lying will help us reduce many years from our lives. We have very few years and we will never get what we want if we only take traditional and difficult paths. Lying is an effective tool to penetrate life in the most intelligent and creative way. This is not based on fraud, but on smart planning and on intolerance with any move we have to take no matter how small.

We live life as if we were in a ring. We want to provide ourselves with sufficient strength; however, a blind conflict that lacks patience and planning will not work. Rather, we must take the position the best boxers adopt. They think calmly and carefully and study the possible consequences of each move before they take it.

Here we control the erroneous beliefs that can lead us to unknown ways. Departing from the self and following fast ways indicate that we lack patience and we follow everything that seems attainable. The temptation that our desires create is not what will lead us to a life where eternal happiness and continuous achievement is impossible. Constant and disciplined control over the self is the one that will take the lead.

B. Distortion of internal content to create adverse effects.

There are a lot of tests and studies similar to that of Doctor Henry Becher, who points out to us the obvious connection between what we believe and what is really happening to us. How can a medicine with a stimulant chemical formula have no effect and become a tranquilliser for some people? Physical reactions are always in line with our mental and psychological expectations. They reflect the chemical reaction that these drugs are supposed to have on the body.

What has really been done in these studies is to make people lie to themselves, that they will be treated and make them believe in their recovery. There is no stronger chemical effect than the chemical composition of positive lying. They lie directly to people. Whoever is taking the imaginary drug is lying to himself indirectly in order to neutralise the drug or create a new effect, depending on what he believes in. Even if you were one of those volunteers, and you knew what they were planning, and resorted to the tool of direct discrediting to yourself, to neutralise the drugs, you will succeed just like what happened with George Dantzg.

We can assimilate the mind to a soft spider's web; it is influenced by environmental factors and it randomly catches foreign objects. We have to constantly clean up what our minds absorb, of thoughts and images from uncontrolled sources. Most of the contents in our minds are nothing more than junk thrown indoors without careful inspection of their validity. Over time, neglect of this process of purification will make our minds more like rings of conflict against ourselves. We will not see things as they are nor will we respond to them with the right reaction.

In other advanced situations, stress and anxiety will be a fixed lifestyle. Hence, the heavy load generated by the random accumulation of information may tear this soft network. Controlling our thoughts will give us the ability to control emotions. Thus, we will maintain a balanced mind in which the process of purifying inputs to remove unwanted objects, is ongoing without interruption.

Two patients had the same serious illness; they were taking the same medicines and were staying at the same clinic. The first was told that he would not recover from his illness, and the second was told that he would be coming out soon. Consequently, they believed what they had heard and what they thought was going to happen did actually happen; one of them came out and the other waited for his death.

From the stories of positive lying: The speed of recovery does not depend on the effectiveness of the drug, but on the speed of the patient's response and acceptance of the idea of healing.

As we see, the issue is about controlling the unconscious networks in the brain. It determines what we feel and then gives us the results we really deserve, which is a clear reflection of what we have imagined. Such unconscious control may be anonymous; its subsequent steps could be unpredictable as well. What it offers us from time to time will be controversial. Eventually, the leading cause of this control is our lack of interest in screening what we deliberately and consciously instilled from the beginning, and our neglect of the purification process of what has been absorbed in our mental content.

The primary goal of the lying drugs is to find accessible paths with which we can take and live, and this is what makes them an effective language programming tool. Through it, we can change any habit or certain lifestyle by reprogramming the contents of our brains; the neurological or mental connections of any habit will be utilised and will die in just a few seconds. At the same time, we will replace these contents with new ones that have positive effects on our actions.

For example, if we offer a non-smoker a cigarette, he will certainly refuse because he pays no heed to that issue. For a smoker, the quickest way to quit smoking is to lie to himself that he is not really a smoker. Just then, the causes and consequences will die.

We just have to not recognise the existence of the habit or the concept in the first place. If we succeed, we will not need to reorient or reprogram what causes us pain or pleasure using traditional long-term methods. We will not need to compensate for the shortfall that we will feel once we have stopped the habit we have practiced for decades. How can a non-existent habit be compensated in the first place? The idea is about controlling the data that is connected with what we do.

One may find it difficult to control his mind. Forgetting or erasing certain things is not easy. This is true because we do not have great flexibility to control the contents of our mind as we control the contents of our smartphones. We will delete whatever images we do not like on our smartphones; we will forget it forever. As you try to reconsider it, you will find that your smartphone will not display it to you again because it no longer remembers or recognises it.

It will be a great advantage if people can control their mind and its contents the way smart devices control their contents or memory. While it is hard to deny the difficulty of this work, we believe in our ability to have a trained mind that manipulates its contents and ways of thinking. As we control the mind of our smartphones and computers, we can control our minds as well; we are the principle controllers and commanders in all cases.

People undergoing treatment sessions, whether related to psychiatric conditions or those seeking assistance for quitting a habit, may follow traditional treatment methods and apply what they have been asked to do by specialists. However, once these sessions are over, it is likely that they will head back to their habits, because they can no longer control themselves. They return to their reality and believe in how much it controls and has an impact in their lives. The period of treatment that guarantees the effectiveness of the drugs is over. Then, there should be another stage of treatment using lying drugs to re-install the basis that was prescribed by the doctor in such a way that guarantees it is not to be eradicated at all. Once you become a professional liar, you can add or remove any habit as if you were adding or uninstalling your computer software with the click of a button.

Imagine if the body of a thin person was stuffed with fat from the body of a fat person, who has been trying to lose weight for a long time and did not succeed. His reaction will be strong opposition and will get rid of those kilograms in a short period because he will discredit the existence of those fats stuffed into his body. His mind does not possess content that indicates obesity and does not recognise the existence of such a concept. This is what will happen as well, if we introduce the percentage of nicotine in the body of a smoker, into the body of a non-smoker. This issue is broader than being confined to one particular habit; it is merely an example that opens the doorway to many other habits and lifestyles.

Once you lie to yourself in the right way that enables you to discredit something that bothers you, you will not need to go to a doctor or a specialist to seek help, and you will not need to read or follow systems that will help you get rid of any habit or thought you want to expel. These lying systems are the strongest and fastest systems to get rid of what is undesirable and are through which we can control our thoughts and mental state very easily.

'Scientific interpretations will disappear; there will be no logic and your physiology will change. What does not happen will happen. You will see what others do not see, and you will feel what others do not normally feel. You just have to master the use of positive lying drugs.'

'One of the positive lying facts.'

This will organise uncontrolled mental orientations, which are dominated by our lack of awareness of things. If we think deeply about what we do, we will notice many clashes between what we do and what we imagine doing. We think about money, and we do not know that what we really want is not money, but what money brings once we have it. We destroy our bodies when we eat too much, thinking we are actually feeding them. Other examples will have other developments and our inability to apprehend certain situations will indicate our lack of understanding of many other situations.

Beethoven was likely to become depressed after he lost his hearing and he thought of committing suicide. What made him continue his life, was discovering his ability to hear from his mind as well, not just from his ears. He managed to cope with music in those circumstances, and he listened to his music well when others thought he could not. Otherwise, how would a deaf person be able to compose music that is well known today?!

As we see, the issue was not just about hearing; what Beethoven needed was to be composing music, so he found an alternative way of doing so without hearing. He directly linked his ability to hear with composing music. His loss of hearing was not a curse. He transformed it into a unique ability that enabled him to compose arts, which others with very good hearing abilities cannot compose.

We are not slaves to our thoughts that we find difficult to control. In ancient times and periods, it became clear how slavery was direct and inhuman; nowadays, slavery is an artificial intellectual limitation, because of the thoughts that have been planted within us for all these years. The sources were not entirely external, but we had a role in frustrating ourselves with our own hands.

In just a few seconds, we can add or erase the intellectual orientations programmed in our minds, just as we do with any intelligent device. It may not work very easily, but by discrediting what we do not want to have inside us, we will extinguish the light on those internal contents. In a short time, they will wither and die.

Possessing such an amount of flexibility in dealing with ourselves and what is happening around us, necessitates that we possess the first motive that will remove the blindness that obscures vision from the eye of our mind, which is the basis of human progress. The real vision is not in the traditional form that we rely on. Animals see but cannot comprehend the truth of what they see because they do not have the eye of reason that we have. The function of our eyes is to see what is behind the images and words and to find the truth of their existence and their future goals.

Smart Discrediting

'I cannot stop discrediting or criticising the usual ways in which most things are achieved. Every time, I discover other finer and more useful ways through which actions can be performed.'

'One of the Smart Discrediting laws.'

Smart discrediting is a similar and complementary step to direct lying; conversely, it is independent and has its own effects and strategies. Smart discrediting depends primarily on our ability to decipher the codes of the adopted practical systems and social norms, and to modify them in a way that serves our uniqueness and creative sensations.

When it comes to smart discrediting, we investigate social norms and the standard process of evaluating them with the aim of ensuring that they have tangible benefits for us. At a time when there are various ideological systems and many ways and means through which we can live, as we cannot ensure their benefits, each one of us has our unique gifts. Hence, we should not trust the common methods and systems of life.

Smart discrediting will help us assess all life systems fairly and cleverly. We do not have to accept practicing all that is imposed upon us, or to follow accepted behaviours. It is our duty to constantly pursue unconventional paths, or at least to truly understand the nature of the duties we perform in our lives. All we seek to acquire in the end is no more than times in which we can find moments of insight, that enlighten and guide us towards our true duties; practices that conform to our potentials, endowments and our unique touches which will transform all actions that correspond with our individual personalities into valuable gifts.

The smart discrediting strategies are numerous. The following are the most important things that you must discredit and the first steps on your way towards smart discrediting.

1. **Discredit what you see and hear, so you are not convinced**.

People often perceive only what they can see, depending on what their experiences and knowledge have provided them. If you ask a doctor about the meaning of success, he will provide an answer. If you ask a servant or a simple worker, they will also provide you with an answer. If you ask a rich man for advice on the best way to get money, he will guide you, just as a poor man will do. However, all answers or guidance you will get from them will be based on their knowledge only, not on the truth.

If you do not know how to get money except by working in any commercial place, your advice for others will be to go and work anywhere. It doesn't matter if your opinion is true or false, useful for those who seek your advice or not, because you said what you really know.

We cannot talk about something we do not know, have not studied or tried before. And no one, no matter how smart one is, can talk about something he does not know, or did not try or get by himself. This is what calls for discrediting the words of others, not because they are liars, but because they are truly honest, but honest with what they know; however, their honesty can be devastating. Others often have little knowledge of the things we want to acquire, and that is the most important thing to be sure of. Experts in the issues we seek to solve or develop are naturally rare, and it is hard to find minds that reflect on the universe in a unique way and above noise and confusion.

When I was young, I never heard my father telling me 'read', neither did he buy books for me to read. It was not because he hated reading or did not believe in it, but because he did not practice it; his knowledge of such a thing was little or lacking. Similarly, a poor man who has little money would love to get more, but he would not know anything about its nature or about the best and fastest way to get it. Therefore, our experience determines how close or how far we are from things, and the quality of what we will provide is directly linked with our experience with it.

Someone once bought a new shirt that matched his favourite colour, brown. Upon returning to his home, his wife saw him and said, 'You look beautiful wearing a crimson shirt.' He was shocked by what he had heard and thought that the seller had cheated on him, selling him worn clothes. So, he went to buy a new shirt from another seller.

The next day, when he went out to work, his neighbour saw him and said, 'What a nice, beautiful, nutty - coloured shirt; it's my favourite colour.' He was surprised by the insolence of the person cheating again. So, he rushed to buy a new one from a third seller.

At work, his colleague saw him and said, 'You really have good taste. I've always liked to wear mocha - coloured shirts.' The person doubted his ability to distinguish colours and went to a fourth seller and bought a new, brown shirt. His close friend saw him and assured him how attractive he looked wearing his new wooden - coloured shirt. He was angry and went back looking for his favourite colour; and he spent his life in the same way.

'One of the stories of positive lying': People have different visions; do not believe everything you see or hear. The colour is the same, but it has different degrees; people also have different visions and experiences.

There are a lot of people around us who wish us good and always give us advice with regards to lot of things. They think they are more aware or experienced than us, and that those who are younger or inferior to them have to take their advice. You would see them advise others as if they know how the course of things will be in the distant or near future. In fact, their advice is often destructive to others, regardless of whether their intentions are sincere or otherwise. The wrong decision, whether it was intentionally or unintentionally made, will remain wrong and will have consequences, either bad or good.

This is what we may inadvertently get from others, since we and those who we receive advice from believe in good faith that what is being said is right, while it is nothing more than a devastating truth. In these cases, discrediting their words and questioning their validity is right. It is rare to find someone with sufficient knowledge about the best thing we can do in all matters, especially if this is related to intellectual, practical and social roles that one must practice.

What you see with your eyes may not reflect the reality in an era where others are capable of modifying images easily. Many people seek to make you believe in the images they see for different purposes and aims. Once you are convinced, you move yourself into a world filled with images and words that you do not believe in and that are not your own.

The important thing about your lack of conviction is to not set limits that do not exist in your life. A free man is not one who believes in what he sees or hears, nor does he let his environment control him or govern his destiny. Health, money, relationships and everything in our life are similar to our ages. You do not know how long your life will be and you do not want it to end early, but you can sentence it to death by jumping off the highest accessible cliff. With regard to your health, you do not know whether you may get chronic or serious diseases or not; on the other hand, you do not want your health to be deteriorated. Still, you can allow harmful substances into your body that cause deterioration in your health. You do not know how much money you will earn in your life. If you are convinced of money - making methods that everyone around you follow, you may spend your great fortune, the amount of which you do not know, in the same way you spend your long life, the length of which you did not know either.

There are two concepts for conviction. The first one indicates that conviction is either a treasure or bondage. Whoever said that conviction is a treasure we own, said this from the standpoint of temporary satisfaction or neglect of the bad conditions that we cannot change, so we can better take advantage of opportunities available to us wisely, without blaming circumstances or feeling that we are victims of time. This is not a bad thing because we provide ourselves with comfort and continuity.

There are a lot of things that cannot be changed and under these circumstances, complacency will be a form of victory. Once you are convinced and satisfied with an unchangeable situation, you will stop trying to hold on to what you cannot reach, and you will give yourself the opportunity to see what is more valuable.

Surrender becomes a triumph when you give up and renounce things you cannot control or get. Consequently, you will not help yourself to find the best in the short or long term, but rather you will give yourself inner comfort and tranquillity. Once you convince yourself that you are no longer interested in something, you will feel that its value is actually reduced, and you will free yourself from its psychological and mental stress.

The second concept points out that '**Complacency is surrender**': complacency here would be more of a surrender. In other words, one is convinced of what is less valuable at a time when he can get the greater value. We often have the opportunity to change what we want to change. Still, when we are convinced of something, we underestimate the value of our actions and therefore our value as well.

Your complacency of what is available to you will not give you more than what you already own at the moment. You will indirectly be convinced that you have got enough of things you want to see yourself possessing better or more of. In other words, you feel a high level of satisfaction in a way that makes you stop learning new things or finding solutions that are more effective.

The one who walks and believes in the words of others and is complacent about his circumstances cannot be listed among free people, because he will be living according to the words and moods of others, or at the mercy of his environment. Those with knowledge know that well; they are good listeners, but they are not convinced of all the ideas they hear because they know very well that people cannot say what they do not know, and few have deep knowledge of everything.

Moreover, not being complacent of what we have is not greed as some people assume. It is just a motivational process that gives us the opportunity to develop our ideas and acquire more of everything available around us. Our lives are not filled with valuable things enough to allow us to live without fatigue or despair. Besides, lack of complacency will help us to stop believing the words of those who think they have enough to live a luxurious life.

Life is full of stories that have always been a source of inspiration to us when we were young. An example of which is the story of the businessman who caused his servant to become rich because of a word. There is also the mother who made her sick son win first place by convincing him that he was healthy and strong enough to compete. Perhaps these stories were not all real, but the events are real and happen in real life without being seen on television or read about in books. By comparing all the events of these stories, we find that those encouraging words were nothing more than positive lies that were told in an emotional, unintended or unplanned for moment. The impact of the positive lie is tremendous on the minds and hearts of others.

'Real beauty lies in telling a lie with a good intention and real ugliness lies in telling the truth with a bad intention.'
'One of the Smart Discrediting facts.'

Thomas Edison's mother did not get convinced easily; she was brilliant with words and at discrediting what she saw or heard. She lied to herself with simple words, convinced herself that her son was a genius who must not be ignored or abandoned. Consequently, she lied to him, and told him that he was so. Because of her awareness of what she was doing, she was able to discredit the difficulties in learning that she saw in her son. She also discredited what teachers and other people thought about him and how he had weak mental abilities.

We are not machines that are modified and programmed easily. In addition, everything that is trying to get into our inner must first go through the phase of quality assessment. This underlines the importance of having filters that can clear fabricated images or information before it enters and settles in our dictionary of knowledge. Eventually, both our skills and cognitive abilities depend primarily on what we hear and see, and every situation we encounter will clearly have an effect upon us. Even small situations, when they are repeated and accumulated, will have amplified impact that will turn eventually into influencing life experiences. Be smarter and make a creative display out of words and images around you and with your full awareness.

2. Discredit what you have learned so you can learn what you haven't learned.

The more you discredit what you have learned, the more you feel that you do not know much. The more you feel that you do not know, the more you will try to know more, and that is a great stimulus for you to learn continuously without interruption. Those who do not learn constantly believe that they know a lot or have learned enough to live in peace, which is why they are indifferent to the continuing process of learning.

There is nothing more valuable that you can do for yourself than learning constantly. Life is not a life without learning. Our minds can bear resemblance to a flower; it is closed in the beginning. Yet, as we learn more, we water it and make it bloom. He who has a closed flower thinks he knows enough, and he who has a blooming flower will insist on learning more. This is mainly due to the fact that if you learn more, the fog around you will gradually disappear. That fog was formed because of your lack of knowledge of yourself and the world around you. Only then can you discover the scientific and practical degree / step that you stand on. People who do not learn continuously do not know on which step they are standing because it is very low. However, once they continue to reach higher steps, the membrane that was formed by the lack of knowledge will gradually fade away. The higher up the steps you go, the clearer the vision will become. From that high place, you will discover how small you are, in the big and infinite world of science.

Science will change your view of the world around you and will remove ignorance that many people cling to. You will see how things change. Things that you used to see as good will turn out to be bad and bad things will turn out to be good. Moreover, you will begin to appreciate the value of many things that you have not appreciated or known their value before. We cannot give our opinion about things we do not know. If that happens, we will be merely making guesses without being aware of them.

Everything in life has inputs and outputs. The human being is just like businesses; he needs input so that he can complete his life. That input is knowledge, without which one would live a difficult and boring life devoid of any kind of creativity. In addition, one cannot change for the better without modifying the information he has or without improving its quality constantly. Those who do not constantly learn and clean their minds of damaged information, will cause that information to rot inside. This will be reflected on the outside in the form of words and deeds.

What is most important in continuing education is not only the valuable information we receive, but the new ways of thinking that will change our lives forever. Our concentration and creativity will increase, and our memory will expand. Only then will we be able to know ourselves and invent new things to think about. Anyone who does not know himself cannot understand the people and the environment in which he lives. All that is happening around him are things that are unconceivable for him; he does not understand their nature. The response will be similar and will not be understood by others or by the universe in which he lives. Therefore, his existence will not have that great value. Certainly, the existence of a lot of people can be viewed as harmful to the universe in which they live. The most valuable discoveries happen when we extract the exceptional and unique values deep in ourselves. These discoveries will offer great power that can increase one's awareness of the living systems. Once these systems are followed, people can live in peace with their natural potential, and we will increase their mental flexibility in dealing with negative incidents.

Our mind will become blurred just like blurred vision. He who knows little does not see or understand things clearly with his mind. Everything that is truly happening around him is doubtful and unclear. This ambiguity will hinder him wherever he stands. The damage that people with blurry mental vision can cause, will not affect others as much as it will strain their shoulders. Dealing with these people can hurt you, but that damage will be temporary for you and permanent for them. The negative doubt here will be a fundamental stage, since all forms of actions and words are unclear in terms of their principle or goal. There is no human action or logical thinking as to what they see revolving around them.

Mental short-sightedness does not only make its victims passive, but also unworthy of practicing any profession. Relying on them even in the work they have been trained to do is not in anyone's interest. Those who have negative thinking and little knowledge are not those who did not receive special education to a high qualification. They are those who don't see the reality of things, they perceive things in life through their negative reality; that is, they have an image in their minds and they want to impose it on most of their dealings and actions, regardless if they are compatible or not.

Once you look at professionals and high-ranking officials, you will find most of them complicated, dominated by a negative view of the world and indifferent to universal principles and human nature. Only then will you find that the quality of education and behavioural programming, which they are used to, is what determines their fate.

Someone with a foggy brain will not appreciate himself or others, regardless of his special academic education. He who has an untrained mind cannot deal with life events whether they are tiny or huge, even if he spends his life in academic study. This is what makes continuous self-education a non-fermentable process. These mysterious laws taught in higher education levels do not affect the soul that is immersed in the mind. Spiritual and mental influences are only the result of living experiences that touch deep emotions and increase intellectual awareness with a spiritual electric blow. Our intention here is not to focus on professions that are taught scientifically, as this is not really related to the overall culture. We are referring here to the mental flexibility and the importance of searching for its real sources to gain as much of it as possible.

We can liken mental flexibility to the membranes surrounding brain cells; each cell in our brain has a membrane surrounding it to protect it and help it perform its function ideally, and the more flexible the membrane is, the more active and connected the cells becomes. Whereas when the membrane or external wall of the cell is rigid, it weakens the cell's activity and its ability to connect to the neural connections. This also increases its laziness and probability of death at an early time. The brain is surrounded with a membrane as well, and with knowledge we will determine its hardness or its lunacy. The more comprehensive knowledge we gain, the more flexible the mind will become. This increases the speed of its connection to its environment in order to translate and process what is happening around it at an acceptable rate. A rigid mind, whose wall is solid, is inherently bad and difficult to deal with. It does not rely on values or principles that govern it and it does not follow a planned approach, rather it follows and debates in a random and emotional manner. Therefore, dealing with a mind like this is a waste of time. It ultimately leads to an inevitable loss.

Mental flexibility lies simply in our brain's ability to stay connected with each moment directly in order to deal with it very quickly. It allows us as well, to link different forms of knowledge and get new creative laws inspired by our thoughts. It enables us to decipher the complex mysteries we face in our social and professional life to have a more flexible life and get rid of those serious and random methods we rely on in our life.

Specialised knowledge in a certain profession or field is not the peak of excellence as many think. However, that is a true thought for those who love safe, effortless zones, as they do not require any radical transformation in personal behaviour or beliefs. In the absence of these transformations, people will lack the values and flexible rules of thought and will become trapped in their current moments and what they see without the ability to expand their horizons of thinking and opinions. Making these changes, which involve many cultures and values that extend from mental flexibility and choosing a field of knowledge to specialise in, will bring about a positive change that can be a source of benefits for its owner.

What we read in books are stories of live events, and what our personal experiences give us are live experiences from which we can learn. When we do not have an ongoing educational and developmental process, it will be replaced by an ongoing and debilitating work that does not have a clear source or an objective without realising that.

'Man is the brightest living creature on earth. However, his creativity does not come out of nowhere; it requires a trained brain. Continuing education is essential to train the mind and to increase its flexibility. Being satisfied with reaching a certain academic stage indicates the existence of a solid mental membrane that obscures the desire for continuous learning. Therefore, you have to discredit the current process, and look for what is not listed in your input list.'

'One of the Smart Discrediting laws.'

We see many people complain about the unhappiness of others, or of their lack of knowledge, while they are actually more miserable and ignorant, and that explains their myopic sight and narrow intellectual potential. They do not consider or evaluate themselves deeply and fairly. They rather insist on convincing themselves that there is no room for doubt in what they have achieved of experience or knowledge. These kinds of people are completely immersed in an illusion that increases the hardness of the membrane around their brain, which in turn obscures the real images. They live in an innovative illusion they cannot see or get out of in the advanced situations. The have drowned too deep in the illusion. They do not see or feel that they are in danger. The majority of the people's opinions are unknown things to them and contract their previous beliefs.

One constantly observes that as time progresses, he feels how little he knew in the past, and as time passes further, he continues to discover that. The reason is that we learn constantly and discover more facts as time goes on, so the veil between different facts and us rises a bit. Consequently, we start to see a certain amount. This developmental process varies according to how quickly one learns. What one learns in years, others learn in months. Some even are satisfied with less. It all depends on one's effort in choosing the pace and quality of learning. While people feel that their scientific mentality is gradually improving over time, many of them lack it, which indicates that they severely lack the constant education needed for self-development.

The majority of what is inside our brains are the final forms of what our environment and parents have craved. We have also participated in modifying our brain. Only then will we begin to see ourselves and our environment with looks that reflect the images' forms carved inside us. Being blind to the idea of reorienting ideas, modifying designs and reducing membrane barriers will make one blind mentally and theoretically sighted.

3. Discredit how you were raised.

What you have learned of intellectual rules and educational fundamentals during your formative years, will not be fair with regard to your original internal roots. Even if the educational treatment applied is good, it will not give the learner his due. Actions and sayings that are suitable for one person might not work with another. Man is inherently different from others. A lot of words and actions had a clear impact with respect to one's psyche and his relationship with himself.

In the beginning of his life, the human being on the inside is like soft, sensitive material that can be formed to create various mental associations that relate to various things. These associations lead to different actions and sayings. Moreover, this sensitivity will form certain intellectual reflections that will be preserved for years to come. You will notice how you start to acquire habits, tendencies and ideas that are outside of your control and are of an unknown source. The use of logic and conscious intellectual trends might not help you get rid of those ideas and habits or forget them altogether. These are merely psychological influences that result from an indirect process of mental programming.

The source that turns someone into an exceptional case (be it revolutionary or peaceful), lies simply in what we learned as we grew up, so we can express what we have held in our chests for years. As we grow up and attract different words and deeds, it will be in our interest to discredit our ideas or question them; the quality of upbringing often determines the fate of some people who fall victims to futile ways of thinking.

People like Doctor Ben Carson are examples of how powerful outside influences can be. They contain beliefs that reflect discipline and faith in the unique mental potential. His mother believed in what we call 'distinctive human capacities'. Her thinking influenced the life of a human being who made people's lives easier and better as far as was possible, and he became a true role model. If negative thoughts obscure and impede the thinking of a child who does not perceive any creativity or natural forces in himself, external changes to that path of dominant psychological disdain will stand between changing the fate of a human being who deserves to see his great potentials and those who will end up lost in a spiral with no end or goal.

Creating a genius educational upbringing may be exceptional in societies full of educational chaos. People raise their children in the way they were raised, and they influence their friends and their whole environment. Those who succeed in discrediting what was implanted in them early in their life have thought deeply of what is best for important people, those who deserve a better life different from the one they have suffered from. The least conscious have to restrain themselves and draw new practical and scientific ideas to bring about new examples.

Some educational foundations are stable whereas many of them are changeable. Later, what was gained might prove to be inappropriate because the times are changing. Moving one educational form to another time and another individual will not be right even if it seemed so. Those born in a different time need other ideas that correspond to their time. This shows that the difference in the environment changes modern interests. In the past, fishing and agriculture were two prevalent forms when it came to ideal and modern lifestyles. The same applies to basic education. Each era has its own different innovations. For example, trying to embrace the skill of fishing and to impose it on a modern world which provides enough of our needs without much effort, will frustrate the creative forces that would have been better used in attracting more consistent ideas for the new future.

The psychological and spiritual seeds, which are planted early in life in order to bring about intellectual changes, carry moral and creative forces that start from childhood. Later, they constitute modern and innovative differences of creative thought. The first process of programming is often the basis of the intellectual rules that inhabit the thought of any human being and that are usually the most hidden. Working to change it is a duty on whoever seeks to explore his colourful roots.

The educational process is almost a psychological process, which looks at the nature of the new creature and at what makes him happy as a unique personality. Once it's found, a great achievement will take place daily. Understanding this process is one of the oldest and most ancient practices. Most of all, what you learned from your parents will not protect you from the vicissitudes of life, nor obscure your obstacles. These scientific and practical lessons are only part of what another person learned in another time. It is rare to find someone who studies his new creation. Those who are aware of this are few, and the probability of possessing those who taught you well at the beginning of your life will be weak. Once you believe that you have found what is useful for you from words and deeds, they prove to be incompatible with your real personality or your present time.

'Parents raise their children with expired and damaged beliefs. Though they believe that they are doing the right thing for their children, they are actually the main cause of their misery. In doing so, they have made life difficult for their children; it lacks creativity and development. So, discredit what you have learned in your youth in order to give yourself the opportunity to enter into a renewed educational process, that serves your goals and keeps you in touch with the latest practical tools.'
'One of the Smart Discrediting laws.'

The reserve bodies that we create from time to time, (which are not the result of our conscious or intelligence), are the result of the past that we return to and temporarily live in by narrating our biography based on previous situations. You are not at your best with people with whom you share a negative past, because the past creates an imaginary character in which you live temporarily. When you meet people you do not like or do not feel comfortable with, your words become harsh, your activity is not at its best, and your psych settles as you control it. The opposite will be true for people who share with you good understanding and who understand your way of thinking.

From all of the above, we learn two important things. First, what we have learned in our youth may be useful to us later in another time. Second, the knowledge that our parents have acquired is limited. It will not serve our duty to our true selves. Instead of teaching, we find that releasing negative energies is an educational method for many, which would hurt all parties. In order to arrive at a correct discrediting process, filter out what you find suitable for you and for your time, and then get rid of those useless appendages. In addition, in those moments you will have given yourself more keys to other doors that will bring you buried and unknown gifts.

4. Disbelieve your imaginary roles.

The role you play now may be far from being the result of an idea of your conscious choice. Most of the roles chosen are not real but are derived from the illusion in our minds. The tribulations that most people face, are the result of their wrong choices regarding the practical role assigned to them. They believe that once they continue to practice and learn many other roles, they will find physical and psychological strength.

In the early stages of development, there is no real interest in the role one has to play and as the years go by, one begins to be confused about his or her future, which must involve familiar skills. We cannot think of mastering a particular role without knowing what that role is. However, the majority tend to play a role assigned to them without thinking about its type and without reconciling it with their unique mentality. This move will undoubtedly lead to psychological and physical devastation. When the mind is not committed to clear training, on a role leading to a stage where tangible results are the basis of its choice, one will move away from what he really cares about. His status as a human being will change to that of a machine, which interacts with the external parts and links the goals of others with what he is continuously doing.

The roles that we are often forced to play, are mostly actions that disrupt the peaceful soul and the creative mind, because they compel their follower to adhere to their rules. In case of departure from them, they will ensure the elimination of our fate. By discrediting those actions and taking a step a little further away from what is apparent on the surface of tempting imaginary roles, we will enter a world that presents us with a challenge in the beginning. However, over time we will begin to recognise the roles that will make our minds at the height of their activity. Feeling pleasure as a result of real work is evident in our inner roots.

It can be said that everyone has one role to master, and most importantly, one's true ability, at first, is to choose that role and the skill that follows. The common methods people follow are either to take advice from others, or to stress themselves and to force them to engage in several roles to finally find what can be called the final role; which is the work that brings pleasure and wealth.

The process of discovering the role must be flexible; it needs patience to seek the activity that relaxes the soul and pleases the mind, not to mention the value that will be added to our lives. Before we begin to think and search for our innate role that will unleash our unique skills, we must first consider the three types of roles: physical, cognitive and creative roles. These stages will explain the hierarchies of roles adopted by the public. Clarification of these stages will help you identify whether you are pursuing imaginary roles that must be discredited. Imaginary roles are all around us. They entice many with some prizes that might look tempting at first. Once you adopt them, you lose your sense of self - worth.

First level: **physical role**. This is the weakest of the available roles, and the most boring. These roles do not need thinking for realisation, but only physical effort. The physical role is mostly common among young people, because they do not have enough knowledge and experience to move themselves to higher stages that contain knowledge or creative roles. This means that those with little knowledge monopolise these roles, regardless of their ages

Basic needs tempt these people to join this hard-working class. Although this stage is often temporary, it takes a lot of time and frustrates us when we do not find those who value our potential or allow us the level of initiative we deserve. Therefore, we see the person of that physical role moving a lot, in the hope of finding what meets his psychological and material needs. He never knows that he would rarely find what he is looking for.

Anyway, there are not many benefits to someone who is busy playing the role of the hard working regardless of the many years he toils. These roles have a routine and a fixed character. They do not give those who play them more than they already had in the beginning. When you examine this kind of role, you find that the one playing it consumes his body only for long years. His creative and innovative mind does not have a role in what he does. What he practices is a job that he has been trained to do for a short period to eventually become a daily routine, which is rarely visited by changes or developments.

Those gullible workers have a very modest message. They only want stability in life, no more and no less. They do not have academic backgrounds that can put them at a higher level, where decisions are usually taken. Thus, they are forced to stay in a static position without thinking about career development measures.

Satisfaction has no room in the hearts of those who have physical roles. They wake up burdened and exhausted daily to perform their boring tasks. They always think that the imbalance lies in what they do, while in fact it lies in the way they think; they have no ideas that make other professions better or that would interest other people. In fact, those who do not have ideas that are possible to adopt, will not draw the attention of any party and will remain alone fixed in one place.

'There is no logic in practicing any job that would make someone just a machine. This is not appropriate for man who was been honoured with his ability to innovate. In the meantime, the most merciful innovations are those machines that took the place of many labouring jobs that men used to do.'

'One of the Smart Discrediting laws.'

Physical work is important. It has always been the foundation of life. The body was then one of the most important things that people could depend on to find the necessities of life. The intellectual orientations of people in ancient times included works that could only be accomplished, by drawing on the advantages of the body such as rapid movement and flexibility in organisation. They used their bodies in fishing, agriculture, mobility, reproduction and even wars, which are essential to living.

Even today, the strength of the body is still a priority for many menial jobs. However, this is gradually decreasing because of the continuous development in e-business, which is taking the place of the workforce. With time, we are depending less on the hands and bodies of human beings. Still, no matter how much we evolve, we cannot dispense with man in many situations.

In addition, what reduces the amount of physical work in the present time is its conflict with time and space; in the sense that no matter how smart and strong the body is, it will not solve mathematical problems, make aircraft or develop traditional means of communication. These things are part of cognitive and creative roles only. There may be no need to tell stories of those who took the path of physical action; once you look around you will find many of them, and we will continue to see them wherever we go.

In sum, the physical role in this modern age will only make those who adopt it a machine, whose operations will take a consistent approach that does not change. Whenever the body is damaged, he seeks to repair or treat it. The best thing that can be done is to take a scientific step that keeps the body healthy and makes it easier to do business in modern and innovative ways.

Second level: **The Cognitive Role**. This role is a combination of physical and cognitive efforts, using both mental intelligence and physical effort. Cognitive roles contain competent characters who have a good knowledge of what they are doing; they have carefully studied the profession they are performing scientifically, and now they are practically applying what they learned in the best way possible.

This role is the most prevalent now. Obtaining knowledge in a particular profession has become quite easy. Even those who have taken the path of physical work are now trying to learn a profession that meets their needs, in an attempt to get enough specialised science in a field and master a particular profession. This transition is tempting for some people because of the high rank it can offer or the better salary that would be sufficient for some entertainment, instead of being blocked from it and only paying for basic needs.

Cognitive roles are limited by nature for two reasons: the first reason is that knowledge is limited. The more you learn the more efficient you will become at work. It is uncommon to teach someone the steps for mastering a certain profession and then expect him to have skills for other professions. In other words, cognitive roles have been programmed to be fixed, and they have ignored mental flexibility in many other respects. This may not be a defect or fault because both the cognitive and physical roles are close and similar. Both depend mainly on physical effort. The cognitive role takes things a step further and studies the parts and components of what is accomplished by hand in a scientific and detailed manner. In the end, we do daily routines and are satisfied from the inside about our knowledge of our work. The increase in information does not mean we can steer away off the specific script, in order to accomplish the required task, so we should not be tempted to go beyond the scientifically and practically recognised limits.

The second reason is the great difficulty in securing high positions. Few are the ones who were able to do anything significant after they became busy with cognitive roles. The limited knowledge that we have under the cognitive role has an impact in making the achievement of tangible things difficult. However, it is not the reason that has the final say in the matter. Moreover, when we hold on to a cognitive role, we work according to fixed rules that are not our own. Releasing our deep creativity and skills hardly ever succeeds because we are under the control of people we work for. The common law in cognitive roles is that only capital and business owners have the right and authority to add new rules and developmental laws. Thus, our creative and fascinating ideas are under the control and mercy of others. They take into account the cost and the time needed to apply our pending ideas. This is not to mention official laws that might need modifications, which are a risk to business owners in themselves.

'The cognitive role will not turn us into machines, rather half machine. To perform this role, it's doer must rely on both knowledge and effort. This is similar to the development of the primitive mechanical machine, which does not rely much on artificial intelligence, or on making it smarter and more efficient by adding elements of electronic advancement to its components.'

'One of the Smart Discrediting laws.'

In fact, the possibility that we submit to authoritative powers is greater under cognitive roles. Standing alone and going after fixing your goals in these areas, is like painting your favourite colour on top of the colour of those with higher authority, and this is unacceptable. Many employers like tyranny in setting laws. They are willing to suppress any objection that would threaten the fate of their non-objectionable ideas. At the same time, we do not have the right to blame them. Those people have worked hard in organising their ideas and in renovating their projects. Most of the time, they have the right to exclude what might place their businesses at a lower level; and if we had a clear feeling that we have brilliant developmental ideas, standing alone would be better than looking for someone to support us. Most of the time this proves to be the perfect solution. Our ideas here do not set strict rules. It is difficult to dim the colourful light in others in order to accentuate our own. This is the same for someone in power. He stands in the face of any attempt to rebel against his actions and rules, which he has long sought to achieve.

Exceptional cases that reflect how this system works exist in extremely small numbers. Someone in great power might be convinced with his brilliant doctor's idea about making a partial change to the work of his existing systems. However, that would be in alignment with his own goal's interests and not in those of the doctor in the first place. Your ability to make partial changes will happen, in the best condition, inside cognitive roles. In order to perfect your creativity and to demonstrate your real value to the public, you need to declare your complete independence.

At this time, people stand in queues in order to get a cognitive role. They think they will find someone who will appreciate their uniqueness and creativity. This has become a culture to the people of the world. The moment you rebel against this system, you feel the risk of sacrificing your future. Those around start asking you to think carefully about your rebellion and retreat from it. Since the number of people are rapidly and continuously increasing, the safe zone has become more important. Jobs are limited and so is income. How fast you find a seat has become a real issue.

Third level: **Creative Role**. The creative role combines the cognitive and the physical roles in form only. Those who play this role study and work, but their goals are far from taking a normal form, which we usually find in cognitive and physical forms. Creative roles rely on deep imagination that create inner images of great projects that have yet to occur.

We can say that what these roles carry of creativity is beyond one's ability to predict. Those with creative roles do the most creative and developed actions. These actions are often their own invention and creative innovations that are usually unexpected or referred to before. Those who follow this kind of role are not traditional and do not care much about the adopted laws. They surprise you with their amendments to common rules after they make sure they are in their favour and in the interests of others. They also possess abundant knowledge and a great and deep sense of the immediate and distant future.

We will not be exaggerating when we say that their achievements can be outside the limits of nature. They do not refer to known laws, but rather draw in from creative and innovative imagination that we witness turning into reality. The number of people who have been able to own creative achievements has been very low in the past centuries, and even in the last few decades. As life evolves, the number of creative achievements increases and becomes more complicated until they end up having many sections. In fact, science comes with knowledge and it facilitates the next process of innovation. The better the ideas of human beings are, the greater the possibility of future developments for future generations, which illustrates the importance of creative work.

A creative role appears in every development case; from creating new systems and living rules, or by inventing a machine whose concept was fictional in the recent or distant past. Indeed, without creative achievements that have been growing for the past few decades, we would not have imagined even the most basic and current developments, nor our uses of these developments. Two things stimulate development work: an in - depth study of something, or a quick developmental idea. This means that creative roles are not for those who possess an innate gift in a certain field; they are also available for those who have worked hard and deeply studied a certain field in order to develop it.

Getting into the initial stages to get a cognitive role can help you in moving on to a creative role, as many do. They possess high levels of specialised education; some people believe by doing that, they can get others to listen to them and apply their unique ideas within the framework of formal and strict laws. However, they actually want to have a deep understanding in a particular area to give themselves the opportunity to invent their own laws and theories.

This process does not involve innate skills and may not call for any, but it rather requires a profound study and intensive effort to reach a cognitive role. The human mind has the ability to study and understand complex actions. It does not require more than conscious thinking and deep concentration skills. This is available for all people, even for those who are thought to be deficient from birth.

It is clear that many of those who followed this approach were initially inspired by their natural inclination towards what they wanted to spend many years studying, and that was what motivated them mainly. On the other hand, there are those who find it insurmountable to search for their natural talents. They are confused by the idea of extreme danger steering away from the safe path adopted by the public. Therefore, they feel excited about the idea of specialising in a field where the probability of securing limited future results is greater.

This means that in order to get a creative role, you may be first required to conduct a long-specialised study, or alternatively you can declare your independence from any official entity and create your own creative roles in your own way. Indeed, creative roles are far from being dominated by limited formal laws and rules, because they are roles of unlimited creative ideas. In order to take the first step towards creativity, you must first develop your thoughts and expand your perception so you can have a flexible mind that is not firm or rigid by nature. Those who move towards new creative achievements are always aware of the importance of having a trained mind that helps them facilitate any possible difficult situations, a mind that does not complicate things or frustrates fantasies and new promising ideas.

'The issue is no longer related to a primitive machine, nor to sharp industrial intelligence, but to a machine that is similar to a soft material that can shape itself the way it likes and that can do what it wants. The vast limit of the most flexible and creative of machines is unpredictable; it is the human mind when it decides to act.'

'One of the Smart Discrediting facts.'

Most of the time, those development ideas that enable their owner to have a creative role are the result of a strong desire to end the suffering caused by inefficient regimes. They can also be the result of a desire to improve what is good. No matter how happy and satisfied we are with the period of development that we live in now, moving forward with it will change our conviction about it. This is the function of the creative role; it does not meet the basic needs of the current system but seeks to develop it and create more effective systems.

Creative achievements have degrees and distinct differences in value, depending on their type, purpose and creativity of its owner. Moreover, creative achievements are not determined by the intensity of their impact or the difficulty of achieving them. Each one of the small or large developmental activities fall within the scope of creative roles, and the least influential of them still shines on the majority of cognitive and physical works. Many creative activities are derivatives of other creative achievements that come to us in new forms.

What is important in the end is settling and organising our creative ideas so that we can find a final destination for them while discrediting the bad ideas that our parents or environment instil into our conscious thinking. Creative roles are not limited to a certain class of people. They belong to those who have a genuine sense of their world and a strong desire to understand and interpret what is around them, in an attempt to build on it and improve it.

The one who boldly got out of the usual methods of physical and cognitive roles, will not find it difficult to live their life differently. He does what fills his life with pleasures and a sense of self-worth. Our sense of inadequacy will not fade unless we boldly and intelligently do activities that can reveal the power of our inner world, which is filled with unique mental perceptions. The value of achievements reflects one's value; what we offer on the outside demonstrates the quality of our inner ideas, and the time we have will never stop us from taking this opportunity to reveal our innovative work.

Charles Darwin challenged the environment that made him sway on roles that did not match the creative role he was looking for or felt inside. During his expedition on the Beagle, he was able to extract creative forces from inside him whenever he had the opportunity to do so. He was also able to get rid of his emotions about things, and to become gradually the most influential owner of a creative role. Aristotle was uncomfortable about staying in Plato's school. He took whatever knowledge he could and watered his mind with flexibility to be able to keep up with his own path, until he had a memorable, unconventional creative role.

Our innovation of our own roles comes from our deep understanding of our environment and its needs, and from a real desire to develop and discover what is not existent at this time. This step cannot be achieved before first looking at ourselves and feeling the creations of our unique spirit. People who do not have a real sense of live things around them and who do not contemplate them, are far from having a creative role and from reaching an advanced stage of their natural potential. There is nothing called coincidence when it comes to having a creative role. Everything comes from our conscious planning, deep feelings in things and our desire to make life's paths easier and more sophisticated.

The following are strategies for getting a creative role. It simplifies your steps as you progress towards your creative roles, arranges your fragmented ideas of different actions and presents the conclusion of anyone who has sought an innovative role.

A. Gain mental flexibility through comprehensive knowledge. In the early stages of our existence, we do not have enough knowledge to distinguish the creative achievements that we can accomplish; that is, finding what corresponds to our innate nature in relation to our tendencies towards certain actions. As we grow older, our emotions unfold. They control us and push us to do things that do not meet our real needs and those of others. At this stage, we are mentally frozen because of our lack of knowledge that would clarify to us, human values and the reality of the universe around us. The deeper our knowledge and the more different sections it covers, the higher the level our mental flexibility becomes. Eventually, we become able to link different sections of knowledge.

When it comes to getting a cognitive role, your mental flexibility indicates that you are moving away from emotions and you are thinking deeply in what you see and hear, through your discipline and patience as you try to deal wisely with each situation. Anyone who has managed to occupy a place within cognitive roles has worked well to recognise the reality of the components that shape and govern their internal and external worlds and to identify themselves and to see the cosmic laws that their world experiences.

This step is always primary. It moves someone from a physical or cognitive role to a creative one. In the beginning, the mind is confused, and ideas are fragmented. Neural connections do not relate to each other with vigour and flexibility. This reflects lack of focus and a weak vision that result from lack of knowledge. By collecting knowledge and facts about various things, we improve mental flexibility through which we can process what we see happening around us quickly and easily. This explains how the physiology of the mind can be easily influenced by the written or verbal information we provide it with.

Moreover, our view of those who suddenly change their situation and start to have a cognitive role won't be confused when we realise the reason behind this sudden transformation from a state of stagnation and dispersion to another of flexibility and creativity. They replace the distorted lens with clearer ones and go through a sudden self-awakening call that deepens their perception of themselves. This also changes the route they have taken in viewing and analysing things. Our creative actions reflect the value of ideas in our minds. Therefore, when we adopt this strategy as a first step, we indirectly extract exceptional values that are deep within us. We express these values by implementing and transferring them to the outside world.

When we have the ideal mental flexibility, we will not stay prisoners inside the current developmental process. Our special cognitive circle will expand and allow us to see future developmental stages. We will see how this is a process that draws its strength and gradually expands its horizon based on previous input. The more we focus on it, the more it astonishes us with new achievements that no one has seen before.

B. Nourish your emotional senses.

Our deep senses have always participated in everything we invent or develop. It is well known that necessities make people strive to do more new creative actions. The senses that fill some people's hearts make them realise those needs and seek to fill any shortcomings. To possess deep emotions is to have an open heart that meditates the world, feels the needs of other people, and recognises the advantages and disadvantages of current systems. Those who do not have deep emotions cannot sense what others feel, and the voices that seek help come from people who do not appreciate the help they are given.

Being a highly emotional person does not mean you have to live your life governed by your emotional reactions without prior thinking. You have to deeply feel the thoughts that occur in your conscious mind and to move them to your unconscious mind. From this principle, you will help yourself understand actions you are planning. The more you mix your emotions with what you are doing, the more powerful your influence on others will be and they will feel your influence in the same way. Once you have a clear sense of what you are doing, your confidence in the success of the business you are seeking will increase.

Our achievements will be as huge as we have allowed ourselves to feel. Therefore, when we have such feelings, we uncover the existing veil to examine how much impact we can make on ourselves and on others. All of this happens before we even start to work. With our feelings, we can really break the time barrier and take a farsighted look at the conclusion of our work. Logic has no significant role in this process, and our senses will lead us while taking reality into consideration. This phase will not only increase your emotional intelligence by which you can know what people feel but will also help you increase the accuracy of your speculations in long-term and short-term plans.

Children usually have deeper emotions than those who have passed childhood. Many of those who have done creative work did not have sufficient scientific knowledge or did not even train their mind to be flexible in and aware of future planning ability. This explains how a child who does not have sufficient knowledge can do better than a specialist and be more excellent in a short period of time, unlike the specialist who spends several years to reach such an excellence. Such a child has deep feelings that enable him / her to sense the world and its adopted laws. This has moved this child to the creative stage without the need for complex scientific grounds.

Louis Braille was creatively sensitive since he was a child. In early January of 1812 just before he became three years old, he helped his father at his workshop in welding metal and making saddles. Although such a dangerous job was not appropriate for a child of his age, his father did not realise this and neglected safety precautions. Consequently his son, Louis, had a disastrous accident. His left eye was deep wounded by scattered segments of wood and nails, and he lost his vision. After several attempts to treat his nerve infections, he lost his other eye and became completely blind.

As the years went by, Louis did not lose his sense of creativity with the loss of his sight. He felt that there had to be some wisdom behind his hopeless condition. No one at the time appreciated or cared for the needs of the blind. At that time, it was thought that a person who lost his sight was also a person who lost his mind, and such a person could not learn or come up with valuable actions to the world that he could not see. This idea stirred anger and resentment within Louis, so his mind tried to find solutions and imagine their applicability. What motivated him the most to create something that could get him out of his ordeal, was feeling compassionate for someone who had the same feeling and like him, who wanted equality among all.

The common method of teaching the blind at that time was to use large letters and numbers that can be read by touching them. However, Louis found this way inappropriate because of its big size and of the slow and difficult task of recognising these letters. He started to draw in his mind a picture of what could make the learning easier, faster and more efficient. Finally at the age of twenty, he succeeded in devising a modern method that allowed the blind to read and learn quickly and easily; he turned the letters into small symbols that stand out on paper, making tactile reading as effective as visual reading.

Louis would not have been able to create his own creative work without his own sense and passion, which was strongly directed at all those with the same condition. In collaboration with his inner senses, he managed to empathise with himself and others. Then he used the strength of his feelings, which enabled him to invent his creative work that changed the course of history and the lives of those who lost their sight.

We can imagine the process more deeply with our emotional senses. We can move ourselves within the parts of this process using both our feelings and mind as if we are part of it, with an aim to reveal its true components in the end. Our logic is not enough to rely on for most of the time and in most circumstances. Logic gives us the correct interpretation on which we base our work; however, our senses take us beyond this limited reality. Senses enrich us with an open and flexible heart and mind that sense the human needs and make them the base of inventing creative works. Thus, we obtain a strong and deep sense of the potential future effects of each work.

C. Examine the surrounding environment: **Detecting deficiencies and needs**. This aspect talks about the development of creative works that have already been created. Many skilled trainees have become more excellent than their teachers by revealing the needs of their future career more broadly and accurately and transferring what they have learned to more distant stages that their teachers were not able to see. At every stage we live in, no matter how much creative work we could reach, there will still be gaps we need to fill, and deficiencies needed by our environment to enrich our civilisation. This is good news for those who believe that evolution has exceeded their ability of understanding complex actions. Perfection has no place in our world and cannot occupy a place in any environment or work. As long as we are passionate about the opportunities that will enable us to create our own creative work, we will always find these opportunities if we direct our minds and feelings at searching for the deficiencies that others need.

Indeed, most people are enthusiastic for any new creative projects. When our creations evolve and result in new products and lifestyle systems, we notice that they change our behaviour and haunt our minds. In the beginning, we were not aware of our needs in order to express them in words. However, when we saw that some innovations would give us a more luxurious, faster and more creative life we immediately removed from our previous systems and moved ourselves to the stage that is most sought. Those who come out with innovations that fascinate us did not only listen to people's opinions, which often do not reflect the real lack, but they also thought of the needs that have no alternative on the surface, and strove to create beneficial projects that make life easier.

Martin Cooper did not wait for words from others to reveal the real needs and invent creative works that did not exist in his world. Rather he worked on scanning the environment to examine the current development of regular communication systems and what systems can be further developed. In the early 1970s, there were no people calling for a small wireless phone that could be used everywhere, without having to be tied up with wires that hindered their movement. As he meditated his environment, which was in strong need of such a project, he had a sense of transforming this project into a proven reality. Indeed, he worked to make his idea see the light and finished his first model with the help of some of his fellow engineers. Since then, the history of communications has changed with his insight, that deeply examined the environment to reveal the unseen needs and meet these needs.

Many creative works were not the result of innate tendencies embedded in their creators' hearts, but of intelligent planning ability that allowed the creators to understand the systems that govern their environment and make the effort to design more brilliant and useful projects. By sticking to your mental flexibility and emotional senses, you will be able to gain great skill in scanning any environment and uncovering its shortcomings. Only then will you trust the course of your efficient and beneficial goals that will not let anyone down.

Every action or tool that was created in the past was based primarily on people's ability to survey the environment, to reveal its deficiencies and basic and recreational needs. There is no need for development and innovation if life is naturally easy and clearly accessible. The basis of all changes and developments that we will see in the present and future is to fill the gaps of unsatisfied needs, and the more we strive to get creative roles the more our contribution will be in improving the form of life that we live now or later.

D. Identifying the real supporter. Not all the support that others show you through many ways reflects the true course of their intentions. We cannot easily identify the place that will immediately support our works. In the final stage of every creative work we create, we may need supporters to help us bring our work to light. The more creative and valuable your actions are, the more supporters you'll obtain. At this point, all supporters call for the same thought, which is supporting your project. However, it is very risky when such supporters are overwhelmed with greed and desire to seize your business and attribute it to them in an indirect way.

Since support can take one form, that is showing interest and directing it toward your business, once you are connected with one of the supporters, you will find yourself involved in actions that control you and your business, and then there will be no room for adjustment or retreat. Many cases of greedy people try to hide their nature with a cheerful face. Therefore, looking deeply at the inner intentions of the supporters instead of the surface words and forms, will reveal the truth of the offers presented to us.

Most valuable businesses need support from those who play the role of mentors and it is rare to achieve success, without any support from several parties. Therefore, choosing supporters will not be so easy and, or, will not always ensure that our business goes well. There are high-cost works and other works that need prior study by specialists to guide us. Supporters sometimes do creative work to support other works. In order to be aware of the real intentions that they practice inwardly and secretly so that they do not show them to their clients, we should understand the systems they offer in exchange for certain conditions, which will make the case more useful and secure.

When you find yourself at a stage where you need support, consider two key things that your business might be based on: money and governing laws. Support for money is one of the most popular laws used by those who support you. What may be a hindrance is not their desire for profit because their support will not last and will stop when their profits start to fade. The real hindrance is that they tend to focus on their material interests and forget or neglect your business rights. In the early stages, such supporters may not show you that, but you will soon notice that some of them are losing the ability to focus on your business because they are focusing on money instead. Those who provide real support, which results in real benefit to all parties without bias to one side, will be a fair choice for us and for our business. Most of the voices that call us to get close to and choose them are not as effective to the extent we want and expect. Profit is the first goal of most supporters. When material goals are in the foreground, the quality of the business will be reduced due to potential negligence that the business will face.

The governing laws will determine in the long term, your ability to control the fate of your business. These laws are legal contracts that will regulate the steps that will form the organisational changes of your business. Most of these laws are not of our own making and can control the actions we have planned with great efforts. Such contracts will be formed to give the supporter optimum returns that include money, power and fame. If we do not plan well to seek the supporter that suits our actions, we will give others more of our exerted efforts than we will give ourselves. We do not have to let others achieve success at our own expense, except when we willingly do so for humane purposes.

Supporters, whether they are independent guides or commercial companies, vary depending on their different values of making profit. Some supporters intend to support the mutual interest of the two parties, while others are dominated by the idea that their success must be at the expense of others. Thus, these values may exploit the efforts of others and reveal the supporters' inner selfish intentions.

At certain times, we often have to be the main supporters of our projects because of the absence and unavailability of basic supporters. To be the true supporters of ourselves, we need to provide our business with ideal people, who help to create opportunities. Support cannot be all made on our own, and creative businesses cannot be completed in the absence of support and joint action from several parties.

Henry Ford suffered a lot of trouble before finding and obtaining his primary supporter. He suffered many years of continuous failure as a result of his disagreement with his partners, whose existence was aimed at completing a creative project. The project entailed manufacturing a new and different kind of light-weighted, benzene car; where benzene was not widely adopted in the 19th century.

Ford lived for a period of time at the mercy of uncommitted supporters during his quest to establish his company. The supporter had intentions that were far from being aimed at fair and successful support. They mainly depended on domination and incorrect predictions because these supporters are the ones who would bear the material costs. At the time he was separated from his partners, he had no chance of getting other supporters because of his reputation as being a difficult person to deal with in this environment. Therefore, he gathered a working group through pre-defined agreements that set the course of his objectives. The agreements also stated that they were not allowed to interfere in his strategies and visions, which had been already thwarted by his former partners. Later, when his team was gathered and completed the installation plant, his creative role began to take its course, and his company became one of the most active and innovative companies in its field.

Finally, when we take a look at the evolution of creative works through ages, we find that it is not always necessary to bring to light what does not exist in the first place. Knowledge entails knowledge, so we can extract developmental ideas from existing inventions or creations. By developing what has already been created, our creative works will be equal to invented works; because our developmental works also satisfy needs and shortcomings and will be estimated and placed within the development process.

5. Discredit what you instil into your body. Imagine the following: You have a machine that operates using mainly natural fuels. Because of your lack of interest in energy issues and lack of knowledge of its resources and importance, you neglect supplying it with natural fuel, and resort to industrial fuel because it also meets your purpose. From time to time, certain parts of this machine will be damaged, and you try to repair it yourself and succeed. Again, it breaks down and you try to repair it. In later stages, the effectiveness of its performance is clearly and dangerously diminished. You start to complain about what happens and try to find someone who can fix it. As the years go by, this machine is completely disrupted because of the damage that resulted from continuous repair, until it stops working and dies.

The ability of energy sources to spoil and destroy is greater and faster than their ability to reform and build. Simple mistakes often lead to major disasters. Proper nutrition needs time, and the construction process needs organised steps. Demolition of what we have built may require only one wrong move. This wrong move is similar to a small spark, which may not be dangerous at the present moment, but neglecting it will gradually lead to a large, uncontrollable fire.

Energy sources have been apparently neglected recently, which threatens people's life. Food is the basis of mental, physical and psychological illnesses. Anything that seems simple can only become deadly poison if used wrongly or excessively. In fact, most of the evil we are exposed to are caused by what we allow into our bodies, which is like a machine that will bring out contaminated and toxic outputs when we insert wrong inputs.

The body is exactly like any machine; it depends mainly on certain energy sources. If its energy sources depend mainly on natural fuels, feeding it with industrial fuel and forcing our body to digest and deal with this fuel will destroy it over time. There is no point and no need to challenge these dangerous natural processes, rather we must follow and respect them, otherwise we will lose them by disregarding its seriousness.

The more we feel our bodies need food, the more we focus on the taste of food and neglect the quality and type of food we must rely on. For us, it does not matter what source of food we eat, but its taste, which will give us temporary pleasure and welfare. In fact, that is the most important thing for most of us at the moment. Food has become more than just a source of energy, and people have created more forms and colours of food. This clearly prompts us to follow the distinctive taste without considering the ingredients of the product, or whether the digestive processes will accept it as a natural source of energy.

It is unwise to nourish our body in a manner incompatible with its nature and the functions of its organs. That is a clear contradiction and an action that is not worthy of being invented by humans, and a challenge to the nature and its operations, which takes a clear and firm approach. The wisdom lies in respecting and accepting the physiology of our body, without forcing it to take a weird course of action that deviates from its basic practical nature.

We pay all of our attention to the sense of taste, even though we know it (sense of taste) is not a true organ that needs nourishment. It is a sense that has been found to help us differentiate between different types of foods and to identify their characteristics, not for pleasure or desires. This misuse of the sense of taste encouraged us to go after our temporary desires, which leads to harming our digestive system, and thus our whole body.

Imagine that you do not have a sense of taste. Would you care for all those delicious foods that you cannot do without at the moment? This will help us and encourage us to choose the best food that is compatible with the nature of our bodies. Lying to ourselves that we do not have a sense of taste will force us to discipline our desires when it is time to recharge ourselves.

This gives us clear evidence that we do not control ourselves and we let our desires control us when we feel hungry. When we eat, we feel great moments of pleasure, and many people stop feeling themselves at that time, which is an act that does not fit a creature capable of controlling his body and emotions.

We can learn from animals and take valuable wisdom from them. Animals go through difficult times quietly without leading themselves to madness, and they have a high level of discipline that enables them to pass through the most difficult times. This steadfastness and discipline do not really require a unique mind, but a heart that makes its holder feel that he deserves to live in the best possible way of living. Without this discipline, animals would not have been able to live for long periods, especially when they encounter the lack of basic (not the tasty and sophisticated) food.

There are many different books and sources that provide perfect food diets. If we want to summarise these books and clarify the basic idea and the end results that we must get, we will find that they all seek to make our bodies derive all essential food from natural foods that can be easily digested. If the body can't find its basic elements, of vitamins and minerals in food, it will not be able to produce these elements. Even if our body is able to produce these elements on its own, it will need our help to increase them. The means of production also need a sound source of energy to continue working. As we neglect the proper nutrition process, some organs will gradually lose their ability to work and will be destroyed in later stages.

Such books that talk about healthy diets advise us to keep our bodies away from the most deadly and harmful substances:

industrial sugar, harmful fats and all non-natural processed foods. These three things may seem little, and we can easily avoid them, but unfortunately, we will find them in most of what we eat. As soon as we eat bread or rice for example, we will be like those who eat sugar. When we eat meat, thinking it is natural, we will find that it is either filled with harmful fats, or processed in unclear and unnatural ways.

These three foods are the most dangerous and have many ramifications that deserve to be well studied. Such foods reduce our intelligence, make us moody, cause atherosclerosis and heart strikes, destroy various organs of the body, lead to brain damage in later stages and much more.

'Food quality is often manipulated nowadays, and we rarely find something natural to eat. Natural products are expensive and not enough for the growing number of people. Even non-processed foods, like fruit and vegetables, are full of unnatural substances. So, discredit what food you enter into your body that you think is healthy, while in fact smoking might be safer than this food.'

'One of the Smart Discrediting facts.'

Commercial markets do not really tell us the content of what we eat. Confusing people or, more accurately, making them aware of what they really eat would keep them away from profit. All that markets have to do, is to decorate the form of their food to make it attractive enough to try, at least. Here, they also use positive lying. If they give a piece of paper that summarises how much damage you will suffer if you continue eating what they serve, they will of course destroy their own goals. That is a devastating truth. It is safer for us to look for the truth of everything we do without waiting for others to do this on our behalf.

The stomach is not a senseless machine. It takes a great deal of effort to absorb the benefits contained in the ingredients we have eaten. It is a machine that can be destroyed and will be less effective if we do not try to make it rest. Only people who don't know the value of their stomach are careless about it. They do not feel and appreciate how important the issue is. If we can see the chemical transformations that occur every time our digestive systems begin to absorb what we have eaten, especially those hard and useless blocks like most meat; we will undoubtedly become more serious about what we allow into our intestines.

Every organ of the human body has its favourite meal, and this organ does not choose its favourite food based on its taste but based on the real benefits that it needs. Moreover, all organs of the body rely on that same smart strategy. Our body cannot be merely called an ordinary machine, but a machine with intelligence far beyond other intelligent human-made machines. There is no need for our organs to speak out and admit what strengthens and hurts them. Scientific experiments have become very clear. It is the duty of every person to know the vital functions of their organs and the nutritional needs of each organ of the body.

6. Discredit your relationships.

Relationships are more than mere knowledge of specific people, but they have a significant impact on the quality of the life we live. It may be a good step to determine the kind of relationships we are currently enjoying. Here, our focus is on personal relationships, which seriously influence our ideas and our personalities.

People in general either support us or burden us, and our role is to determine what we can take from them. In fact, such a step cannot be determined if we lack both social and emotional intelligence. To be equipped with this skill, we are required to study human nature deeply, consider the various human values and principles carefully and study history in which many lessons can be learned.

The greatest ordeal occurs when we follow our feelings and don't study and examine people deeply before dealing with them. Unfortunately, we often fall victim to an idea that is not clear or logical. We might be influenced by a word or a situation before we really think rationally about these words and situations. Thus, the manipulation of words to control feelings has become common, and charming styles have become more important.

If we look at history, we will find many types of people that must be avoided. This means to distinguish the types of people that are most harmful and negative to our lives. Not getting rid of such people will lead us to trouble and conflicts that are not of our own making. People are infectious, and we will be infected by their various nature. Whatever values we hold, there will inevitably be things we can't really control.

One's behaviour may not give clear indications of one's true nature, but rather reflections of the behaviour of relationships one has. This is what can be called reflexive behaviour. If we try to delve deeper into the background we have about most things, we will find that it is not of our own making; most of its internal perceptions have been unconsciously formed in our minds depending on our social experiences. Moreover, discrediting all the negative backgrounds planted in our minds will help us to form images, through which it will be worthy to see our world and whoever is inside it, through them.

Here, we will clarify the worst types of people by mentioning their qualities that clearly distinguish them from others. These people should be institutively avoided. Even if you find out that they are among your closest people, it will make your days more peaceful and secure when avoiding them. It may sometimes be difficult to find out that one of our close associates has one or more of these qualities. However, the issue is not about us, it is about those who abandoned the original human principles and sought an unstable and scattered life.

a. Discredit hypocritical relations. The most serious diseases in the world are not physical as many believe, but mostly psychological. Hypocrisy occupies the first place in the list of the most dangerous and most harmful diseases. The greatest harm of hypocrisy will not be reflected on the one that practices it, but it will affect a huge number of people. There are two types of hypocrites; the first one knows the truth and publicly denies it and tries to distort it in, frankly, audible and visual ways. The second type knows the truth and pretends to support it, but actually fights it from the inside, which is the most dangerous.

If we look at ancient history, consider our present age, and try to find the cause of all the social devastation that happened, such as, breakdown of all relations, whether personal or public, the collapse and disintegration of people, and all kinds of administrative corruption in all levels; we will find that hypocrisy is the main reason. It is a motivational step to spread hatred and revenge, and most importantly, it destroys people's minds secretly. This is what makes hypocrites the most dangerous social category in terms of harming others. They publicly act as if they are the friend who seeks public benefits, whereas they spread destruction and corruption when out of sight.

It seems difficult to detect the hypocritical relationships that do not show their intention to distort the truth as in the case of the first type. Such people master the game of controlling their feelings and facial expressions. It may be difficult also to rely on our emotional intelligence through which we can detect whether someone is a hypocrite or honest, by just looking carefully at their different facial expressions. Therefore, people will most likely believe and follow the phony tracks that were made to serve unethical plans. Consequently, we see a hypocrite's victim defending this hypocrite without clear or logical reasons. These victims are unconsciously brain-washed; they no longer see the truth and do not want it. When these infections spread, they cause destruction at the level of individuals and communities as well.

Who are the most hypocritical classes of society? It may be difficult to define one category without the other; and we will find the hypocritical relationships around us in the simplest classes as well as the largest ones. Hypocrisy is often adopted differently by people in authority. Although it conceals and deviates the truth of such people professionally, there is a way to reveal their truth and focus on their work and history rather than on them personally. This investigation reveals the hidden works behind the scenes.

'**Beware of the hypocrite and discredit all that he says. He is a professional person who is evil pretending to be honest. He keeps you away from yourself and steals your efforts and transforms you into a machine to serve his endless, selfish interests.**'

'**One of the Smart Discrediting facts.**'

We may wonder why hypocrites practice these actions. In fact, there is no obvious reason. It is a habit that has settled in people who have been programmed as machines to be controlled. They have a willingness to practice the worst business if there are personal interests or certain gains. Therefore, hypocritical relations are useless and can end easily at any time. They can at any moment change the course of things from being your supporter to an enemy against you.

There are many tools used by hypocrites to achieve their purposes. Money and science serve hypocrisy sometimes. People use money as a powerful weapon that buys minds and exploits the most urgent needs. They use science to camouflage the facts that would raise awareness of blind-minded people. Money and science are the basis of power in life, and many other systems are derived from them. The issue is not about money, but about what money can do. It fills hunger and builds schools and hospitals. Science can sabotage minds by making false books and spoken words to alter and distort intellectual knowledge.

Perhaps the greatest harm we will get when we do not investigate and keep away from hypocrisy is the loss of our efforts and living an unstable life free of any kind of creativity. We may fancy obtaining results and prizes that are not real. People in general have the ability to manipulate and control each other, and there are many tempting offers that can control the feelings and minds of others. The act of tempting people of winning great results and prizes in exchange for doing an action, needs certain and small efforts that will serve great interests, so this manipulation is a powerful tool itself.

b. Discredit relationships that lead to bad luck. We think that the one with bad luck is the one who lost his money in an unsuccessful trade, the one who suffered a serious and chronic illness, or the one who lost his family in a traffic accident and so on. On the other hand, we do not look at the underlying causes of the losses we have been exposed to.

There are many around us who have been exposed to events and situations that make us see how bad their luck is. However, once we look at the reasons behind what they have experienced, we will discover that they are completely innocent of what happened and deserve all the compassion and support we can offer. Although it is not logical to believe in luck, it would also make sense to say that there is no such thing called good luck. All positive results in our lives are caused by our conscious and planned efforts. Nothing valuable and systematic occurs by accident. On the other hand, the existence of bad luck is logical because it is resulted by random practices that are not rationally planned.

This illustrates the difference between the one who brings bad luck (represented by a variety of problems and ordeals) and the one who is naturally exposed to failures caused by unfavourable circumstances. This is an initial step that we should understand before we plan to move away from those with bad luck. Not all the bad things that we are, or will be exposed to, are a result of our own actions.

The one with bad luck is simply a human being who seeks his best to destroy himself by relying on all the tools available to him. He makes his money a curse instead of an opportunity, and his relationships a burden that take away his happiness rather than being a support. Whether he does so consciously or not, it is the same. This ability to change the course of actions is practiced deliberately, but we call it 'unintentional deliberateness'. This means that we deliberately practice some behaviours that we are not aware of their truth and consequences.

There is a clear imbalance in the planning process of people with bad luck. They want to bear onerous burdens that last for a long time, in order to follow one of their worldly desires that does not last long. The issue is like the debt we are going to get; it seems very easy to get that cash but paying it back will cause us insomnia; it's extremely difficult in reality.

The problem doesn't lie in the burdens these people are carrying, but in the burdens that they will transmit to you upon meeting with them. They have too many problems that they will infect you with. This will oblige you to take on extra burden. What we clearly see is that the misery of people with bad luck is caused primarily by their constant demand for new problems, not by circumstances they experience that are beyond their control. They are not prepared to learn from their mistakes or to correct their behaviour.

'The one with bad luck will only guide you to the roads that will only bring you trouble and will try hard to push you towards the stage he reached; he has nothing to lose. His vision of those who are better than him will generate jealousy within him. However, convincing others to join him will make him feel safe, and that he is not alone at the bottom.'

'One of the Smart Discrediting facts.'

The first thing we have to do to be able to distinguish between one with bad luck and those suffering from harsh and unforgiving conditions is to study one's past to see what his behaviours have been based on, either on indifference or real efforts that have not been fruitful. In this step, we will avoid those who seek to infect us with their limitless problems, and we will be able to help those who deserve our support as much as we can.

7. Discredit moody relationships. We often hear people indifferently say: 'Excuse me, I am a moody person, I feel happy at times and sad at others.' What such people actually mean is: 'I am a weak person; anyone can control me, and anything has the ability to spoil my day, no matter how small. I like to spoil the happiness and peaceful days of others because I have no control over my feelings.' This makes us recognise how they admit their weakness and underestimate such a case as this.

It is realistic to say that no one can control his feelings at all times, and the loss of control over our feelings is one of our human qualities. Nevertheless whatever it is, it is untenable to lose this control to the extent that we lose our minds. Of course, we sometimes lose the control over our feelings in certain circumstances. Even at that moment, we should be able to control it. Moody people like to generalise whatever happens to them by linking small events with many other irrelevant events, which makes their lives chaotic.

'He woke up early in the morning and fortunately, found that he felt happy and peaceful. At first, he smiled at all his family members and neighbours when he was going to work. Suddenly he stumbled upon a small stone. He got angry and lost control, insulted and hurt some people and stayed in his bad temper until the evening. The next day,

he woke up smiling with a cheerful mood, but spilled his coffee on his way to work. He got angry again, lost control of his feelings and spent his day pessimistically. As for the other days of his life, there may be nothing different except that they have different small obstacles he will face.'

One of the positive lying stories: Keep away from the one who loses control over himself; he is spoiled by nature and will infect you with his serious and frustrating mood.

The inability to see the real size of things to appropriately deal with them disturbs our feelings. Moreover, your mood will always seek to get you into a cycle of negligible conflicts. Dealing or living with such conflicts will disrupt our peaceful thinking and reduce the quality of our creativity at work.

The real happiness is represented in small things or moments, like sitting down to watch the sunset, walking under rain, or reading a book in a quiet place. Happiness is not about buying a larger house or traveling to another country. Moody people are an enemy of these pleasant moments that nourish the soul. Losing these moments means losing many moments filled with tranquillity and peace. Hence, do not ruin your mood by accompanying those who love to hurt themselves and strive to transfer their bad feelings to others. Be free to accompany those who appreciate moments of spiritual tranquillity, and the importance of estimating things properly.

8. Discredit gossipy relationships. When you tame your tongue, it indicates that your mind is perfect and balanced. Those who have a creative mind will not have the slightest readiness to engage in trivial matters, especially with regard to the stories of others. Gossipers worry about anything. They are devoid of useful daily activities and goals. Therefore, they are preoccupied with the words of people. They stab people in the back with distorted conversations that are far from the truth and have no value.

Gossipers are the people who feel inferior the most, and this feeling is a great danger to us. Our involvement with them will be like sitting among people who examine our shortcomings and catch our mistakes, to spread them either for fun or to frustrate our efforts. They have a different kind of bad luck; they hurt others and themselves without feeling and have no clear explanation for what they do. The real explanation is that they are not satisfied with themselves, so they occupy themselves with those who are satisfied with their lives. They believe they compensate some of what they lack by doing that.

'Words have magical power; they are not as cheap as it is already known. Words have great ability to change the content of minds and distort the facts to spread corruption, or to create or destroy creative minds. Be careful not only to discredit most of what you hear, but what you say as well, because you do not know how powerful your words are to others.'

'One of the Smart Discrediting laws.'

This is indeed what we see when we accompany a gossiper. His main problem is that he has no useful activities to fill his life. His words show how he is a victim of this age. He has been betrayed and neglected by all human beings, and no one has stood with him to help him regain his usurped rights. As soon as we sit down with those who give us passive feelings, we will set our positive feelings aside and preoccupy ourselves with the passive and fake emotions that they planted inside us.

9. Discredit good circumstances so as not to lose them, and the bad ones so you do not have them.

The circumstances we live in are either the results of our actions or the actions of others. We often find ourselves in a complex and difficult environment that is not our own. If we do not discredit it, then we will believe in it and admit its permanent existence. Moreover, the transition from one stage to another in our lives requires discrediting the circumstances we experience. What we see as good and gentle may be treacherous. What seems bad may be in our favour if we look at its future course.

Since failure is often a lesson and a reason for success, success can also be a cause of failure. If you always face bad circumstances, which you did not make or bring to yourself, you may have to congratulate yourself, because that is a sign of your progress and a great opportunity to come up with creative ideas. This is not in praise of the bad circumstances because they always bring us undesirable things. The most important thing is that your circumstances that you curse, may be a great opportunity to improve your thinking and increase your knowledge. Those who experienced bad circumstances and moved to better ones with their efforts carry valuable principles; they changed what is inside them first and then the impact extended to the outside due to the improvement of their living conditions.

On the contrary, if someone gets something without effort and conscious thinking, he will not be able to appreciate it fairly. His comfortable conditions were brought without study and efforts. Consequently, such a person will not bother to strive to get beyond the present stage. The good circumstances that we did not achieve with our effort will be the effort of others, and whoever gets something for free will give up his freedom and put himself at the mercy and gratitude of others.

It would be very logical to say that if everything we want is supplied to us without effort, we will be greedier and will not recognise ourselves or feel others. As long as we have everything we need, why do we make effort, help others or even think of other things that might bring us trouble, even if such things are valuable? This does not apply to everyone. Anyone who has knowledge of this can make himself a man of values, who respects himself and nature around him. His circumstances will not control him or control his thinking. Every human being has within him a proportion of greed and will not be wiser than animals without discipline. The lessons we learn every day rarely come to us automatically, but we go to them and feel them.

There are two types of circumstances: forceful and attracted. Forceful circumstances are ordeals that are not of our own making, but of the aggression and folly of others. While we are not blamed for these circumstances, our main role at this stage is not to pursue the damage inflicted on us or not to settle in the place where we felt we were victims. Therefore, the fundamental problem is not the circumstances or the people, but our reactions and how we respond to the ordeals that we did not make. Discrediting these troubles does not only mean you are not affected by them, but also you do not recognise their existence in the first place. They are like a strong and cold wind; it is only fleeting and must come from time to time. Given that the forceful circumstances are temporary in nature, they will impose themselves on those who do not understand the reason for their existence and how to deal with them and will persist for long periods.

The attracted circumstances mean that our actions attract the conditions that correspond to them. The actions we perform will receive the appropriate reaction. The source of attracted ordeals is clearly known. We are not sufficiently aware of the fact that we are the reason for everything that is attracted to us. Human nature clearly asserts that no one wishes to harm himself, but one seeks to harm himself because of his lack of awareness of good practices and human duties.

'The circumstances we are facing are not universal facts that don't change but are just times created by our practices and behaviours, which can be gradually changed by our own free will. We can transform our circumstances into a bliss even if we have few resources, or into a hell if we misdeal with them, no matter how great the resources we have.'

'One of the Smart Discrediting facts.'

Comfortable circumstances send the brain messages of stability and lack of effort. Hence, there will be a lack of deep thinking in the creation of new ways of thinking and living. As long as you are stable, you will not do any scientific research and will give up intuition in all aspects of life, whether small or large. External change stems from internal changes, and vice versa. External changes stimulate internal changes of ideas. Most of the time we try to find ways to make internal changes upon the appearance of sudden external conditions that we are not accustomed to. Living in normal and convenient conditions will not stimulate internal intellectual changes or external environmental changes.

In fact, the bad that most people are exposed to is not because of the forceful circumstances and not related to other people, but because of their false thinking that led them to their ordeal and made them live in bad conditions. No one will admit that he led himself towards what he is subjected to. This idea seems far from logical, and this confirms the existence of attracted circumstances. If someone is aware that he is the cause of the loss in his life, he will admit it. However, the one who is not aware of this process will not admit that he is responsible for the ordeals he brought.

That is like a disease. We are often the main culprits of our disease. Every time we get sick, we begin to be confused and complain about our illness, knowing that we could have avoided it from the beginning by regulating the type of food we put into our bodies, or avoid doing some behaviours that are harmful to health. It would be illogical to ask someone about the reason behind making ourselves sick with our own hands. We eat to nourish and grow our bodies, drink plenty of fluids for the same reason, and smoke to feel fun and empty our negative energies. We spend long hours using technology to entertain ourselves. In the end, we do not stop to reflect on the fact that the mean opposes the end, even if we never intend to harm ourselves.

Even those who we see commit suicide do not intend to harm themselves, so how can it be logical? Suicide simply aims at getting rid of pain that is greater than the way of suicide (whether a jump or a bullet), at least for them and the events they have experienced. Every human has his own experiences.

This action is just a sacrifice; smaller pain in exchange for greater pain. Even those who practice harmful habits do not practice them to harm themselves, but for other reasons, believing that they are healthy and positive.

We can compare the conditions to the four seasons; we have to go through hot and cold, and other cool times, and the right action is to control them and create the atmosphere we want. If we feel extremely hot, it is not necessary to mourn. Instead, we can move and find a place that has a peaceful atmosphere consistent with our objectives. It is true that there are naturally many forceful circumstances because life is not naturally easy. However, we learn by failure, take the lessons and derive our strength from sudden unexpected turns. With our true understanding of intractable circumstances and with awareness of our ability not to attract hidden ordeals with our own hands, we will create the third kind of circumstances: ideal and creative circumstances.

In conclusion, the tool of smart discrediting has no limits, and you have the freedom to discredit everything you want, but remember that there has to be a goal behind it, and that discrediting something either means that it is incompatible with your personality and goals, or that it needs to be reorganised and developed. This discrediting is not done in order to rebel against laws that are likely to be wronged by our mistrust. Make the tool of smart discrediting always work in your favour. Your discrediting of systems, events or words does not mean, not admitting them completely, but re-evaluating them and neglecting the useless aspects that do not represent us on the personal level.

Think as a Soothsayer and Act as an Omniscient: Smart Planning

'Whereas the past presents to us lessons we can learn from, and the future causes us tension and confusion; the present gives us the reasons hidden in the past and the opportunity to decide the fate of our future.'

'One of the positive lying facts.'

It might not be logical to confirm that the planning process is part of positive lying because planning is in fact, a group of assumptions and guesses of things that have not happened yet. Those future assumptions are not fully or definitively confirmed; they are merely sketches of events we desire in the future deliberately and consciously.

Surely, no one has the ability to know the unseen, and words of soothsayers are far from reliable. However, far-reaching and deep planning can give you an ability that resembles that of knowing the unseen. Knowing the unseen is a divine ability, which cannot be possessed by any other creatures. However, humans have been distinguished with far-reaching planning, which is a tremendous ability in itself, if used subtly and precisely.

With careful strategic planning, you can become certain that future things that have not happened yet will actually happen. However, knowing the tiniest details of those things is difficult and impossible to happen. For example, you can plan to travel to visit a friend on the date you selected. When you do as planned, you will notice that you have become someone who knows what to do and what will happen in the future. Some small details are unpredictable. You cannot tell if there are things beyond your control and ability to predict, such as delaying your trip due to an unexpected change in weather, or any other similar obstacles that are beyond your ability to predict.

Your careful and long-term planning will resemble having the ability to know the unseen. Knowing somehow what will happen in the future is a kind of predicting the future in itself. You imagine something, examine it thoroughly, and then plan to make it true with conscious efforts. It may seem easy, but the difficulty lies in one's ability to see things from all angles and to anticipate the direction from which danger can come, even if it comes from the narrowest and the most unlikely direction.

In fact, the matter is simple and does not require taking it too seriously. Planning varies according to one's vision and sensitivity to the details. If you are employed in a company where you are paid a fixed wage, you will be able to predict the amount of money you will earn annually. This cannot be seen as a distinctive action because anyone who earns a fixed wage knows well the income he will get in the following year. To be distinguished in planning, you have to draw a more detailed image and come up with the end result of your remaining income for the year by identifying your expenses accurately, classifying them and working out how much of it you can invest. Thus, you will be managing and organising your financial life in a way that relies on thorough and precise planning.

Even soothsayers study the past, present and the hidden ways of human thinking, and then give the results one deserves. They merely plan well and study events carefully. Here, you are not going to need the help of soothsayers. You will be your own soothsayer. The future results we are going to get can often be learned by looking at what we are thinking about in the present. Based on what we are doing now, we can guess what can happen to us in the future. When you become your own soothsayer, even the most astute among soothsayers will not be able to predict what will happen to you in the future with the same precision that you own.

With short-term and long-term planning, you can easily picture your future life and the events you will face. You may not have been given the ability to know the unseen, but you have been granted a similar ability. Not using this ability means that you are satisfied with living a chaotic life void of aims. Being sure of what can happen in the future is something that cannot be fully achieved. We have, though, the ability to carefully plan whatever we imagine. We can come up with sensations and emotions that help us change or modify what we had planned for before.

Those who plan for all the details of their lives carefully are quite rare. Despite the importance of planning, only few people understand it. Future assumptions are long-term insights that depend on what has happened, what can happen, and what would happen as a result. Only those with far-reaching planning and deep insights have the sense and imagination to see future events that have not yet happened. Those events might not be as precise as they had imagined and felt them. Nevertheless, these events often indicate the same end result.

'The hunter, who sets traps for the prey, looks from afar and waits. He then watches the steps of his prey heading towards his trap. The prey sees only what is in front of it and follows its instincts because of its short-sightedness and inability to see beyond reality. It does not question what is happening or assume what will happen. Thus, it ends up having a miserable fate. The hunter looks at his prey and laughs at its ignorance and inability to predict the future. One should not think that the prey is just an illiterate creature. The prey can often be a human who foolishly falls into the trap because he did not pause and speculate over the matter.'

'One of the positive lying facts.'

The number of mines or traps that life has set for us is very big, and many of them are around us. However, this number will not matter much if we have the ability to see beyond what is visible. For everything you see, there is often a cover or a layer that hides what really matters to you. This layer will shortly become transparent and will allow you to see what is greater and more important only if you take your time looking at it and thinking about it.

As a human being, you will never want to walk like a prey and fall in any hole hidden under a little bit of straw that can be easily detected. In fact, you have to look at everything around you and at all your actions until that cover becomes transparent, and then you start planning again to get rid of those mines you did not know existed.

Be sure that anything you have not planned to do or to be part of will turn against you in time, if not in the short - term then no doubt in the long - term. We plan for a reason; to draw our future goals and thus our lives in full. If we are living a life full of activities and things we had not planned for, that would certainly be the result of actions imposed on us by others because of our way of thinking that lacks planning. Eventually, the end result of these actions is useless to us because they do not reflect what we are passionate about nor show our real potential.

The majority of those who have future visions and broad planning take an offensive position while being far from taking a defensive one. This means that those who constantly plan for their lives will have new goals and visions. Then they will be able to face the world with those visions in mind in order to communicate them to everyone and everywhere. Those who do not know what it means to live with careful planning will live most of their lives taking a defensive or emotional position. They are always depressed and fearful, and they do not know the real reason behind those feelings. Moreover, dealing with such people is confusing because they do not know themselves and are played upon by others, so they end up as victims in most situations.

Here are practical steps for a smart planning process that will help you shape your life strategically and accurately.

a. Study the past and the present. When you study the course of events both in the past and present, you will have the ability to predict future events accurately. Once you get back to the past moment of a certain matter and then look at how it is functioning in the present, you will be able to predict its future possibilities. What is happening now is the result of what happened before. Future outcomes are influenced by what we did in the past, especially what we plan to do in the present.

We will surely face many complexities. In order to plan well and make the best decisions, we must study the past and the present of everything we face. This study must take its due course. Things do not change as quickly as we expect them to, and the present - what is happening now - is somehow similar to the future and can provide a possible indication of it.

There are laws for everything in this life, and when we study these laws well, we will feel that we are in control. Past laws are weaker than the ones we have in the present because past laws are further away from the future and are expected to give us weaker prospects. However, past laws are still important and that depends on the issue we seek.

For example, when you want to have a future glimpse of your relationship with someone, take a short trip to the past to see their past actions with others. This will give you sufficient evidence of who they are. However, because the past has passed and people are changing by nature, we must not rely on it completely. In this case, you had better resort to the present since it is clearer and more reliable. A person's nature in the present will be the same in the future. Even when some people are spontaneous, partially hidden or unclear, their actions regarding insignificant things can offer strong evidence revealing their future reactions to many serious matters in life. When someone is emotional and cannot deal well with unwanted behaviour, he will certainly not react well to slightly larger things.

Each time you encounter a mysterious thing that is difficult to plan for, start studying its past and then focus on its present. Study its nature, how it used to function and how it does now. Then, make your plans taking into account the results obtained.

b. Stay away from the bumpy roads that others take and get familiar with unique and easy methods. When we plan for something, we face many paths. Some look easy and clear while others appear to be difficult. However, appearances can be deceptive and hide the opposite of what is clear. If you are planning to get $1 million over the next two years in order to start your project, you will find many who recommend that you work hard all year long or get a high-paying job. To them, this is the easiest way. However, you can simply borrow it from someone within a few minutes. In that period during which you intended to work hard for years, you would save yourself a lot of time and effort and earn double the money you borrowed.

The easy way here does not refer to having a rest, being lazy or taking risks. Life is difficult and bitter by nature. These easy paths, referred to here, are not completely easy. They are simply less difficult than others. Difficulty has different degrees. Thus, in the previous example, you chose the easiest and most convenient way. When we fully understand something, we may choose to follow a lifestyle that may appear to be difficult, but in fact it is an easy one compared to other available and normal lifestyles.

We often take the paths that will ultimately lead us to our goal; however, we neglect the type and quality of these paths. This is similar to food. Eating is the only way to satisfy hunger. Here, you will be taking the easiest way to reach your simple goal of feeling full. As you ignore the type and quality of the path you are taking, you will not focus or care about the type and quality of the food. Therefore, you will choose the difficult path unconsciously or unintentionally. We can apply this to almost everything in life. We all plan to be healthy, rich and intelligent, and we seek to achieve that. However, eventually we forget the right ways or methods that contain basic laws that can shorten our path.

c. The gift of insight. Everyone has been endowed with a natural gift, but it might exist in varying degrees. To help improve and strengthen this gift, one has to identify it and study its nature. We all receive messages that can be real visions that transcend the present and reveal events in the near and far future.

What makes visions so important is that they are truly real and accessible to anyone. The soul has receptors and senses that receive information from its surroundings, and then they send it to the mind to form a vision for the future. This is a clear transition from the conscious world to that of the unconscious. We receive the information consciously and send what concerns us to the unconscious. Over time, this forms future visions related to matters that concern us.

Certainly, not everything you see in your sleep is important, but you have to identify what you see in your dreams. To do this, first look at the clarity of the sound and the image. The clarity of what you see proves the truth of your vision, whereas random and incomprehensible dreams are often worthless. One important sign is when we feel that we are living the vision as if it were real, not just a dream. The second thing that indicates truth in your dream is your feelings. When the clarity of the dream is not enough and when your feelings are real, they will inspire you and reflect what will happen in the near or distant future. Your visions are often related to things that concern you only. Your soul has senses and receptors that only accept things that interest and concern you.

You may think you do not have this talent, or that you have not had a true vision before, and that is true for many people. Therefore, what you need to do is to develop this innate talent. To develop anything, it takes training and focus. As for visions, you just need to think about the matter at hand and believe in it for a few seconds before you close your eyes. Visions are often encrypted, which means that half of what you see in your dreams is a vision while the other half is just a scattered picture. You may see things that are worthless, but in the end, you see signs of what matters to you.

d. Depend on your intuition and trust it, as it gives you a glimpse of the future. Intuition may also be a form of vision. The difference is that you use intuition while you are awake. Intuition is used and felt by the general public, whether they know it or not. We often feel it is important to avoid or fight something, or that things have happened or will happen. What is closest to the heart is often closest to reality.

Some of the situations that happen to us seem to ring a bell of something inexplicable. This feeling is a reflection of images that reveal mysterious future events. At the same time, we get a feeling about something happening in the present or the possibility of it happening in the future. Relying on your intuition, you will be able to see what is hidden from you in the present time using an inner feeling of coming events. Thus, you will be using your intuition to deal with encrypted information and events that are not easily detected now, but perhaps later in the future. Things are usually revealed over time. Even the simplest hints that you sometimes get from your intuition may give you a sincere future vision, which can help you forget about the difficulty of the moment so as not to be imprisoned within it.

To have a truthful intuition, you need to use conscious thinking that is based on realistic planning. Your intuition will help you in the small steps you take in the present, in order to give you the ability to plan to what is further in the future. This does not require magic or anything beyond human nature. Our intuition is a unique ability that was given to us within a certain limit like many other abilities. Utilising this ability can bring us great benefits. Even your ability to read these words now and understand them is a unique ability that you have been endowed with. The moment your brain cells are taken away from you, your ability to think will be rendered useless. You will lose the ability to think and understand what is going on around you in the present moment. At such a time, you will forget the fact that you were a human being only five minutes earlier.

When the brain is working at its best, intuition works faster and will seem clearer to us than ever. Similarly, when our mood is clear and stable, it will stimulate our intuition to act involuntarily. It is difficult to describe intuition using words to someone who has not experienced it before. Our intuition works best when we are in the company of those who are close to us. When we feel reassured and peaceful, our telepathic abilities will enable us to see glimpses of the future. More importantly, the images they provide are clear and almost completely visible.

Furthermore, we cannot choose what we see through our intuition. Your intuition is designed to help you see the best ways to go, but that might not always work since there are other factors involved, such as circumstances, the environment and an individual's ability. Even when you are capable of seeing the most powerful ways and methods, you might have to take other roads due to circumstances. What matters here is that you have identified the road that is 'less difficult', you have recognised what is truer than truth itself, and you are willing to head in that direction once you have the chance.

e. Always use new formulas. Long-term planning needs continuous adjustments because things change, and unexpected events happen. There is nothing fixed or unchanging no matter how long they take; therefore, be ready for new and constant modifications. Many people ignore the possibility of unpredictable events while planning for their goals. As a result, you find them react emotionally rather than modifying their plans confidently and calmly. This is inevitable when we do not ponder over what might happen in the future.

New plans or modifications can be made easily by keeping an eye on the continually renewed present. For example, one of the long-term goals to lose weight by eating specific foods, will quickly change when you discover that new foods have proven effective in eliminating extra weight. Here, you will start making adjustments to your plans, without messing with your final goal.

Continuous modification of your plans indicates continuous development. When you modify something, you show development and improvement and that the previous idea was not as effective as the new one. Successful goals are often the ones that are constantly modified and developed in accordance with their nature and needs. What is interesting is that small things often have a great impact, so simple changes to your plans will leave a positive effect, will make things easier for you and will bring about whatever you have been waiting for.

f. Stay committed to your plans until the end. Commitment is crucial because when you steer away from your plans, you abandon everything you have worked for and everything you might have gained in the future. Even if that was temporary, it would still mean you have to let go of everything for a while. The negative aspect is that you do not know what time might bring. You might forget things, lose your fired passion or lose a valuable opportunity. In the end, this can be fine if it is not your own choice but that of the circumstances around you.

You certainly cannot give up something whose results are consistently apparent to you. You will stick to your plans and goals as long as you see fruitful results. However, that may depend on the nature of your projects. Gradual results are not always possible for every goal we seek to achieve. Imagine you are building a new house. Each time you place a block you will notice the difference. This tangibly proves that you are achieving your projects gradually. Edison's attempts with the light bulb required patience and planning. The results of such attempts may not appear today, this month or even next year. However, when the results come, they will be like someone who has finished building his new home, but this time instantly not gradually.

Break the Time Barrier

'Time is not a real thing; it is rather a modern innovation that we have created to organise our lives and activities. It will not be impossible or illogical to modify time to slow it down, accelerate it or even stop it. Everything that can improve our lives will exist, and if it does not exist, we will create it.'

'One of the positive lying facts.'

It is not possible to measure time accurately, and the constant estimates we see and live according to are built, in fact, on a regulatory basis to realistically simulate time. Our contact with time varies in degrees and measures. The estimated speed of time passage is not the same for all people; these time transitions reflect either pain or pleasure. One minute can be felt to be a very long time during unwanted times, whereas good times pass in the blink of an eye. In both cases, we ignore the content of real time, and we live with our immediate events without preoccupying ourselves with the usual interpretations of time.

When time passes within a clear, fixed, scientific approach, it does not mean that we all perceive it in the same way. Time is different in its concept and speed for each one of us. How slow or fast time passes depends on what we do and what happens to us during that time. Time does not bring us tribulations or benefits; it is our behaviour in that time that does. By breaking the time barrier, we are able to experience ideas and actions that are compatible with our nature.

The concept of 'real-time' is philosophical, whereas 'time' is a physical, scientific concept. Real-time always has a starting point and an end, so we always say: 'Let's meet at 10 am', or 'Let's leave at 5 pm.', or, 'The meeting will start at 11 o'clock and will continue until 12.' The meeting, thus, has a time limit of one hour according to our estimates. However, time is limitless. There is no starting point or end. There is no difference between one million or one billion years because we live reality only in the present moment. Actual time is the present; there is no past nor future. You can compare the difference between time and real-time in the following example: the moment you start watching a show or movie on your smartphone, you press the 'start' button and you will be able to see how long it will take. You realise there is a beginning and an end for what you are going to watch. This is real-time. As for time, it is when you see a live show; there is no starting point or end. Time is thus a universal force that brings us together and provides us with continuity.

The concept of real-time as temporal estimates will be of great importance because it helps us organise our practices and activities and thus to better use our potential. In this way, we will have the ability to recognise the passage of time, so we would manage our time and finish work efficiently. This will ensure that we are accurate and fair in everything we are involved in. Ultimately, this is tightly related to our choices and our ability to manage our time. And this is not easy to estimate especially when it comes to managing all aspects of our lives and to achieving our health, psychological and material goals.

On the other hand, with respect to health and geriatric experts, there is criticism of the misuse of people's temporal estimates because most people measure their age based on the number of years currently adopted. In this way, they do not die but kill themselves without knowing because they measure their ages according to the temporal estimates of those who get sick and die early. Someone in his fifties would thus think he is at risk of becoming ill, and someone in his seventies would believe death is near. These are but thoughts that attract illness and death, even when they are unlikely to happen.

There are many other examples that result from faulty temporal estimates, which control many aspects of people's lives. To act wisely, one has to live life with a different perception of things, even if he seems to be the only one holding these beliefs and even when they are contrary to common public ideas. Everything in our life is personal even in things we believe are agreed upon. What decides the fate of anything is the way we perceive it and deal with it, rather than the rules and rumours that are spread in magazines and newspapers. Hence, we will need to start creating our own temporal estimates that are in line with our values and goals. Then we will not have a short time or a long time but rather 'an infinite period that is deserved'. This would give us enough time to deliver our intended messages to the world, so they would flourish and appear in the best form possible.

That is basically what we can do to break through the time barrier; we have to deal with direct events and situations and follow their path instead of that of time. Time is something relative and it is something we create. In order to control time in a way that corresponds with our lifestyle and interests, we need to depend on our creative strategies. The main factor that can actually change time and the real content of time is our actions. Through our actions, we can change whatever we see and live, and consequently we can decide whether we attract pain or pleasure.

Based on this personal perception, we can tamper with the programming of time in a way that serves our interests and goals as well as many other reasons. We have different personal characteristics, and we want to control the speed and concept of time, so we can live in the time that we deserve and that is in line with our uniqueness. By controlling time and changing its concept individually, we are able to arrange time and make it serve our projects wisely and justly.

Every action has its own temporal speed rate. For example, an hour of playing will feel shorter than it actually is, whereas an hour at work will feel like a complete hour. An hour of pain and sadness can feel much longer. Our physiology has something to do with this. We affect and are affected by our neurotic cells. This in turn, affects our psychology, which can either give us strength or frustrate our passion.

If you want time to go fast, do things that shorten the sense of time, but if you like to make time pass slowly, do boring and tiring work. You may find that sleep makes time go too fast compared with all other fun activities. Those who sleep a lot do not only feel that time is running out quickly, but also they live the time and the dreams they want.

Having this ability, you will be able to live in any age you want. You will also be able to create your own history, whether in the past or the future. An hour can become a minute if you want it to be like that, and it can last much longer than that. We can surely make time serve your interests and goals creatively and justly.

Abraham Lincoln made a year feel like a month, and a month feel like a day, at least for himself. That made him a very patient person when he tried to reach his fate. When you go and read about the truth of what he was doing in those thirty years, you will find that they were not thirty years to him - they felt much less than that.

If Abraham had known that his success would take more than thirty years, he might have paused and replaced his goals with ones that could have been achieved in a shorter time. Messing with the concept of time helped him endure all those years. This is an ability we all possess. All we need is patience in order to reshape our quickly - formed beliefs that are based on common notions.

We may recall a time in our life when we were waiting for someone, and when they were late, we convinced ourselves they would arrive shortly. Every time we were about to lose our patience, we would tell ourselves again in consolation that they were about to arrive. Finally, we realise that it had been an hour or more and we hadn't felt that time. However, had we known the waiting time from the start, we wouldn't have had the willingness to wait or be that patient.

This is what has happened and will happen to those who have long-term goals; they delude themselves of a near end although they know it is really far. They push themselves to be patient by ignoring the fact that time is running out and that they are becoming rapidly older, as they go after goals they do not strictly know the future of. Thus, such people seem to mess with the fixed concept of time and make themselves feel secure so they can become more patient.

Breaking the time barrier will enable you to live life in the best way possible regardless of the environment around you. Your aim might be to have fun and comfort and not just to head patiently towards your distant goals. Some may think that having a special lifestyle in which you distance yourself from the way others live can alienate you from your surroundings or reality. This cannot be true as long as you do not move away completely from your time. You can live in a time that had long passed and move away from the development we partially live, in order to become someone who appreciates a simple life and finds pleasure in simple things. Abandoning your smart devices might seem weird in an age where people do not communicate directly anymore. However, as long as this can make you live a humble life where you can find pleasure in simple things, instead of big things that consume your body and mind, you will have achieved something different that brings you comfort.

The day you were born was part of your fate. You did not choose that date because it was something out of your control. However, living in the time you have pictured in your mind is what you can control. This is not achieved through physical transition, but rather through cognitive and mental transition. We do not have to follow and match all that our time brings with our personal values. We have the choice to follow whatever our souls desire and our minds choose.

Centuries ago, many thinkers foresaw our present time, and all their written or imagined predictions anticipated most of what we see today. This proves that man can see and even live in an age that is different from his own, using his mind and perception. Many people around us still live in ancient times and are too distant from reality that only few people can reach. The French writer Jules Verne, foresaw our time and almost lived and felt it centuries ago. He internally lived in it, but he was externally trying to adapt to this time with all the means and tools he could use, to bring that long awaited and distant time closer. He often forgot to eat for several days. For him these days felt like hours not days. His ability to control time was not a coincidence. It was the result of his flexible thinking that could reverse all the usual perceptions and create non - existent or visible intellectual and temporal systems.

Verne broke the time barrier with his visions about the advent of light, which would later make cities shine in times of darkness as if the sun was at its highest. He even went further to stress that man would be able to fly away from earth and explore the distant space one day. He also hinted to other inventions that would help make social networking operations easier among people around the world. He was also able to recognise those regions around the globe that are difficult to reach, especially the depths of oceans.

Verne did not only see what we can see now, his theories still predict events that have not happened yet but are expected to in the future. As we wonder about the kind of abilities that enabled him to reach such an academic stage where he could make all these predictions, we conclude that these predicting abilities are more than just ordinary speculations. They reflect his ability to reflect on the human feelings that connect different sciences and truths. Only few people are capable of using this ability. His predictions were the result of organised steps towards what man can achieve with his mind, which is gradually developing over time. He achieved this by thoroughly studying his own psychology and stages of mental and physical development, as well as identifying his endless, potential limits.

In these situations, we can act as if there was no time in the first place, and we can live with the current situation and view it with visual systems, that can capture all the observations and fine details in order to create more useful patterns. We can imagine the future fate of these observations and seek to attract all future things that appear unrealistic, in order to do them in the reality of the present day. Feeling that time is limited and too short for our goals and personal lifestyles, will confuse us and force us to take an easy and guaranteed path and keep us away from bold changes.

Those who reject the evolution that we are carrying out are not necessarily reactionary or people who do not like evolution. They simply do not see their happiness through those new behaviours, and they are content with the simple lives they are living. By living in the time you deem best for yourself, you will be distinguished by being someone who lives true to himself with beliefs he has chosen, and who does not let himself be a victim of the prevalent and modern programming. Every human being will eventually choose for himself the time he is comfortable with, whether in the past, the present or the future.

The strategy for breaking the time barrier involves two levels: a personal level and a public one. Breaking the time barrier on the public level aims to clarify the effects that can be caused by the ideas of the individual in his time and world. On the other hand, breaking the time barrier on the personal level increases the possibility of developing creative energies and personal values to live an unconventional or unlimited life.

1. The Public Level:

Studying the stages of scientific development. Studying how human beings have gradually progressed with their innovations and what mechanisms govern their development, will give us the ability to see the dimensions of human potential. Man has moved through time constantly evolving different lifestyles. This transition relies primarily on our unique ability to create new and easier lifestyles in order to eventually eliminate the old-fashioned methods of living and the habits that prevailed in the past.

By contemplating the stages of scientific development that our ancestors have undertaken in the past and which are still adopted and will continue to be so in the future, we understand how the development system (which consists mainly of organised steps of work, learning and innovation) moves people to break the time barrier in which they live, in order to move to a more sophisticated and wise era.

We are living in a stage which highlights the importance of breaking the time barrier, so that we could rely on an evolving mentality that would head constantly to what is better. When we remain in our times and rely on specific traditions and lifestyles, we show a rigid mentality that does not aspire us to modify the rules that govern our lives, and this does not fit our thinking and evolving nature. Therefore, breaking the time barrier (by studying the basic rules upon which the stages of scientific development were based), will give us new insights inspired by our ideas in order to understand the process more clearly.

This can be compared to any educational approach. At first, we study the basic rules of any scientific topic, and then we gradually move on to the more complex, advanced stages. As we go through all the stages and understand them well, we will have no choice but to add new ideas and insights by linking all the forms of knowledge we have acquired previously. As a result, we can transform all previous processes or stages into realistic and understandable assumptions in easy and enjoyable methods. We will also multiply the benefits acquired from innovative new laws.

Tampering with the imaginary future. When something is distant or still has not been applied yet, it will seem to us unrealistic or more of an illusion. However, once we carry it out we will gradually be disillusioned, because by then we would have identified the realistic rules that govern it. To tamper with the imaginary future, we have to gain the boldness that would enable us to break out of the usual systems and design unprecedented building structures.

Everything we see now of technological, social and other developments were mere illusions in the past, and many people who tried to predict them were being accused of madness because what they said and dreamed of was beyond the limits of human capacity. One day, no one believed that the earth was spherical, and the idea of human ability to fly was completely illogical. Believing in the possibility of travelling from one country to another in a period shorter than that from sunset to sunrise was often seen as crazy.

Therefore, every time or age has a specific expiration date. Nature does not determine that date, we do. We will continue to keep our advancements and we will remain the same until someone bold comes to tamper with the imaginary future and look at what is distant and mysterious in the future. When we break through the time barrier in this way, we do ourselves and everyone around us a great service.

Today, tampering with the imaginary future is not quite new and exciting anymore. Many people are continuously doing that in order to evolve. That is why we have become used to seeing new innovations that emerge every day. This phenomenon is no longer as dazzling as it used to be, in the last century or even before that. However, the fact that we have many inventions everyday does not mean that we live in an ideal time. Many shortcomings are still unknown to us. If we saw what our ancestors thought in the past when they were presented with new ideas that seemed unrealistic to them, it would be clear to us that what we are witnessing now is not that brilliant and that evolution is not limited to a specific age or individual.

2. The Personal Level:

Select the speed of time that matches your nature. With this plan, you can control the real content of time and determine how fast it will go according to your own lifestyle. Many of us have given up certain goals and actions because they require a lot of time, or because they will make us live boring and difficult lives. Determining the speed of time means adjusting its content in accordance with our nature and our goals. We can either make time our loyal servant or an enemy that creates obstacles because we fear losing it.

There are many personal lifestyles and goals that are not accomplished because of the fear of the time they need, as well as of potential future risks. If we study the lives of all the figures who were responsible for changing the course of history and the way of life that we live in, we will find that they acted as if they had the ability to change the normal course of time. Therefore, such people spent many years working on projects that seemed intolerable to most people or appeared to be outside of the comfort zones that people like to stay in, especially in the early stages of life.

Our efforts need sufficient time in order to turn them into tangible successes. Moreover, as we control the content and speed of time, we tend to depart from social norms that rarely add to personal benefit. At the same time, we will learn to be as patient as possible. Intelligent and conscious planning has to control the fears that tell us we are wasting our time in unsecured endeavours. In the long run, we will realise the time we have been able to exploit, by controlling its core content in order to make it a server for the messages we want to deliver.

Smart Practice. Stick to modern innovations that are compatible with the nature of your spirit and practice them, even those innovations that seem strange and deserted. Abandon the innovations which do not match with your spirit and goals, even if they are widely accepted. The goal of smart practice is not to follow everything that enters our social life, because by doing so we abandon what distinguishes us from others.

There is no need to be attached to all the ideas in our surroundings and communities as a whole. Practicing what is compatible with our unique innate nature is more important than allowing everything that is new into our lives. The issue here is not about accepting or rejecting evolution, but about the psychological and mental repercussions that we will be affected by, because of the tools we depend on. Every new tool that is created has a big role in changing the behaviour of people, and every innovation we allow into our lives changes our behaviour, even when we think it is unable to do so. This is like swimming against the current and thinking it will not pull us away.

When we accept to be content with new social norms and laws and with all innovative technological tools, we will distance ourselves from many of our original values. Not all new things will have a positive impact on us or help us organise our lives. Two decades ago, social communication did not used to be as it is now. It was quite different as it did not rely heavily on electronic messages, because there were no smart devices that facilitated such processes and made them necessary. These devices are things that usually have advantages, but their disadvantages exceed their advantages because of the complexities involved in them. As a result, people have lost many of their human values.

With smart practice we do our interests and goals a great service, just as Lincoln did. We do not just control time, we make it work in our favour by living our time peacefully and by attracting realities that match our unique nature. This is one of the qualities of the richest people in the world. They have a deep sense of their own selves and exploit all of their potential, which has become obvious to them in addition to their ability to control time. Smart practice means doing actions that match our characters and that bring us the greatest benefit possible. It also means not allowing ourselves to be victims to new inventions.

There must be times in our lives that we love and cannot forget, not only because of the tools we had at that time but also because we felt internal peace. There is no need for your behaviour to change if the time you live in changes. The times you spend passionately with yourself are the most important. Live with yourself and to yourself in the time you imagine internally and externally and feel all the small and big things around you. Do not live waiting for things you do not know when they can happen. Living a life like this is filled with anxiety and endless tension.

Commercial Positive Lying

'Commercial markets that do not utilise commercial, positive lying are like a fisherman trying to catch a fish without a bait.'

'One of the Commercial positive lying facts.'

Try to listen to these offers and hear them instead of just reading them:

'We are the best.'

'We are the strongest.'

'We have credibility.'

'We have generosity.'

'We are safety.'

'We are the most beautiful.'

'We are the fastest.'

'We are the finest.'

'We are the most economical.'

'We have what you want.'

'With our services, we will take you to the top.'

'With us, you will guarantee a bright future.'

'We will guarantee you the job.'

'We are aware of your wishes.'

'Buy one and take the second for free.'

'Buy two and take the third for free.'

'Buy with $100 and get a $20 coupon.'

'Buy our perfume and become the most charming.'

'Our mobile phones will enable you to do the impossible.'

'Buy our products and get a free gift.'

This age has become filled with offers and ideas that are difficult to track or even understand; therefore, it seems difficult to follow simple methods that lack ferocity and boldness. It is very likely that we will lose the profits of our creative ideas if we do not enter that crowd and promote our ideas with great courage. Technological development seems to have made life easier for us, especially in the world of commerce and marketing; however, marketing has become more complex and difficult because there are many competitors with many skills that we lack. In fact, that evolution did not happen in order to help a certain group of people only or to facilitate things for all people. Only the wise would understand how to use all these sophisticated tools in a clever or a usual way.

In order to stay as far away as possible from inferior positions, we must equip ourselves with the best knowledge of how to market ourselves and our ideas. That is often complex as it requires a lot of effort to come up with ideas that can make us beat those who are better than us, or at least make us approach an ideal level that will distinguish us from large crowds.

We all see how the majority of companies repeat similar statements in different words. If there were actually one or two of them that can be seen as the best, then they would be lying to us in an attractive and legal way. Perhaps what they produce is the best according to their standards and capabilities, but it does not mean that what they offer is the best ever. Everything we see in commercials does not reflect the truth most of the time; nevertheless, the words or images they use give them great support and ensure their continuity.

There is no commercial institution, no matter its field or kind, that does not rely mainly on commercial positive lying in order to increase its profit. This constitutes the basis for temptation and a study of desires and needs. The lies that are practiced in the world of commerce are not for the purpose of deceiving you but for convincing you. If they succeed in convincing you, you will believe that their products are the best and you will be satisfied with what they are offering you; and at the same time, they will have made their profits.

You might have heard about the experiment of the Russian scientist Pavlov, when he used to ring a bell before feeding his dogs. He made one of the dogs very hungry and as he brought him food, he used to ring a bell. He repeated this every time he served the dog food. After several attempts, the dog immediately drooled when the bell rang, even before food was served to him. The dog's mental associations had been tampered with. Pavlov had made the dog react to a certain action; he had programmed the dog to associate the ringing of the bell with the time of food.

Since that time, this experiment has expanded, and it continues until this day. However, it is no longer applied on dogs or other animals, but mostly on people. This experiment represents profit policies for companies, and it is used as strategies to increase fame and profits.

Positive lying relies primarily on the exploitation of our visual and auditory senses. With time, we form mental connections that make us run after all that is new to satisfy our desires and needs. This is Pavlov's approach to animals, which was conveyed to us in a clear manner. That experiment can also be successfully applied to us. In fact, there are many things we share with animals. The physiology of many animals is quite similar in some respects to human physiology.

We see how ads are characterised by different and deliberate music to make the product or service more appealing, by directly influencing our emotions. When we are certain of a benefit in something, we will spend lots of money for the sake of what stirred our emotions.

Commercial lying targets the most sensitive parts of man, his feelings and fantasies, which are often difficult to control. So such lying always outperforms man's limited rationality.'

'One of the Commercial positive lying facts.'

All that is related to the world of trade and investment uses commercial positive lying and relies on it in a way that cannot be underestimated or abandoned. Commercial positive lying is the basis for the success of any service or product. Only those who don't want to successfully communicate their ideas to the world would want to abandon positive lying. If you look carefully around you, you will find that every banner or logo uses the law of positive lying. The laws and ideas of positive lying that we will mention here constitute only a very small number of what we might find wherever we go, because each marketing process has its own innovative and unusual strategies.

There is no benefit from a distinctive idea that no one knows about. The power of promotion used in the world of commerce is measured by the strength of commercial lies. When we see our favourite actor, singer or player using a product we have never heard of before, we will approve of this product and purchase it. This is just one appealing style among many others.

We live in a world that is full of ideas and innovations that come to us every day, and it has become difficult to communicate our ideas easily to people. By trying to break through the crowd without some attractive marketing methods, we will waste our efforts and our ideas will be ordinary among thousands of ideas around us. Therefore, the issue is no longer about releasing an idea in the market, which provides a lot of other alternatives; it is rather about creating irresistible images in the customer's mind. This motivation is the first thing to be planted in the mind of those who will pay money for ideas they like.

Most marketing offers are intended to tempt not to present the actual truth. No one has the slightest willingness to admit his flaws. Showing or admitting the existence of some basic flaws might leave quite negative influences in the customer's mind. This is not that serious, so we needn't get angry. Our world is incomplete and there is nothing flawless. It will be certainly negative for manufacturers or service companies to point out the flaws in their products.

Commercial lying requires three strategies, without which we will not succeed in finding a place for our ideas in trade markets. The following are the basic strategies and steps that give commercial lies influence in trade markets.

a. Indirect Marketing. Imagine you enter a restaurant and after you have chosen the meal you wanted, you read a sign saying, 'We do not offer one meal only. Two meals are the minimum number of meals you can buy.' At that moment, you would begin to wonder at how rude and greedy this restaurant is. They want you to buy two meals instead of one to get more profit, so you go to another restaurant because you do not like to deal with people who are trying to exploit you in this immoral way.

You enter another restaurant, you order your favourite meal and certainly there was no obligation to buy anything extra. When your request is ready, you are surprised to find that you are given two meals instead of one. When you go to inquire about the reason, a staff member says, 'You are right. You ordered only one meal, but we love our customers so we serve them another meal for free.' At that moment, you would feel quite happy with the generosity of this restaurant and you would decide to come here instead of other places.

However, after you go home you look at the bill and discover that you have paid for two meals instead of one. There is only one difference between the two restaurants, and that is the expression used. At the first restaurant you were explicitly asked to pay for something you did not want, and in the second one you were given the same offer, indirectly.

Commercial positive lying is a marketing process that is inherently indirect and can never be straightforward because it would uncover some purely profitable trends. All the marketing subjects taught are in fact nothing more than sophisticated and intelligent deception strategies that do not seek to harm people, but to convince them to buy the product of a certain company or to request some effective service.

Even most of the offers we see encourage us to buy, by offering us something for free or a discount if we buy at a certain cost. Indirect marketing methods make us feel that we are winning and see ourselves saving money. Nothing is given to us free of charge, and even the discounts that we witness from time to time are part of marketing and are simply part of a process of profit reduction, aimed at achieving a larger profit in the future. In fact, these strategies are not immoral. Think of what might happen if trade markets used straightforward marketing methods, just as in the example of the two restaurants. Commercial positive lying will surely be more considerate and rational to the trader and the consumer alike.

When Nestlé first tried to introduce one of its products into the Japanese market, it faced some difficulties and complications. There were plenty of products, not to mention that the Japanese preferred their own products to imported ones. Thus, the company studied the Japanese market carefully and discovered that 'KitKat' was very close to the Japanese word 'Quito Katsu', which means 'good luck', which is what mothers say to their children before going to exams. Thus, the company found the way that it could bring its products into the market.

The trick initially consisted of free distribution of a mysterious type of chocolate in a red packaging, that contained no writing and claimed that it brought good luck to anyone who ate it, especially students who had exams. After a few years, the mysterious product gained a positive reputation. The initial method was simply a prelude to an indirect marketing process. What Nestlé did was that it indirectly promoted its product in a way that did not harm people or subject them to fraud in any way. It changed the concept of the product in a way that caused happiness through the new mental link it formed in the minds of those new consumers.

b. Exploiting Man's Five Senses. Everything we see and hear about in the commercial world does not result from a random marketing process, but rather from an early and accurate study of human nature. People are different by nature. Some of them are influenced by what they see, others by what they hear and some of them by what they taste or touch. Therefore, this study takes into account the strengths and weaknesses of each individual; if someone is influenced by what he hears about, another is influenced by what he sees. Thus, those who are affected with what they see will not be significantly affected by what they hear.

This is an innate issue. People's visions are clearly different and cannot be the same in all aspects. In other words, the image we see is not seen in the same way by other people despite being the same image. If the commercial world relied only on images in advertisements, it would not be highly effective and the marketing process would be insufficient.

We all see how each product has its own special shape, colour and distinctive name regardless of its type or quality. For every service, there are offers that make use of attractive images and phrases. This is what guarantees the success of marketing and promotional campaigns. If words do not work, attractive images can present a tempting alternative, or even trying the product before buying it. This is the main reason why commercial positive lying does not rely on one or two senses only, because there is no guarantee that tempting the customer will succeed in a world full of similar ideas and similar tastes.

Although cigarette companies are no longer using commercial lies as they used to do before, they are still making huge profits because consumers are the ones lying to themselves. Smokers let their senses motivate them to buy cigarettes continuously. They associate smoking (despite being negative in itself) with positive associations that would bring them happiness or comfort. This applies to any other commercial product. We might not need it, but we have associated ourselves with it. Therefore, abandoning it will be difficult and will leave empty spaces in our lives.

c. Hiding Additional Charges. This might be one of the strategies that irritate us the most. It makes us feel as if we have been robbed. Some might even consider it a form of positive lying that harms people. The good thing is that most of the time we do not encounter such a thing, and we are not required to pay additional charges apart from in some cases.

Additional charges here are not in any way similar to loans people borrow from banks. If people do not repay the loan in the agreed period, they can be sent to prison, or their property might be taken away from them. This is another immoral action that is made appealing by using negative lying. We will discuss this in detail soon. Additional charges are rarely harmful and usually come in the form of very small expenses. At the same time, if these charges were not hidden, a lot of problems would emerge because of little details, and people would end up avoiding many valuable offers.

Sometimes additional charges are equal to the price of the product itself, or maybe higher. Not hiding these charges would encourage customers to avoid buying the product because it would be clear that what we pay for the product is much less than the additional charges and fees. This is what makes hiding extra fees quite important. Failure to do so would lead to losses and would deter people from paying for something they think is exploiting them, rather than entertaining or benefiting them.

'We go around trade markets without any intention of buying anything, but we come back carrying big shopping bags. Eventually, we realise that we have been victims of appealing offers, and that in fact we do not need most of the things we have bought.'
'One of the Commercial positive lying facts'

Therefore, the act of inventing qualities is more important than the qualities themselves. Many products pretend to have certain qualities that they do not have, in order to convince customers to buy them. The products marketed in this world claim to make us stronger and smarter while others claim to give us pleasure and luxury or beauty and elegance. The list is full of endless, tempting offers.

Damage caused by Commercial Positive Lying

Sometimes commercial positive lying becomes negative when ethical principles of sale are ignored, and the material aspect is highlighted. In general, commercial lying that relies on tempting promotional campaigns does not intend to take people's money. It is rather an infinite tool of excellence that seeks to highlight one idea among many other ideas. If we think carefully about this, we will realise that no one would force us to hand our money to them in exchange for a certain product or service. It is voluntary and we decide how we will spend our money.

Therefore, the problem does not lie in the marketing process itself, but rather in the way we respond to those offers, which will make us imbalanced in managing our money and unaware of the difference between what we desire and what we really need. Responding like this will motivate us to follow our desires and encourage us not to manage our money. Thus, we will end up wasting our money on things that bring us pleasure instead of real benefit. Then, we will have made commercial positive lying a burden and it will become a threat to our money, due to our inability to manage our money well.

On the other hand, commercial positive lying will turn into a negative and unethical process, which involves fraud that will hurt people. It will try to control the way we spend our money for a long time without taking into account our different spending capabilities. Commercial positive lying does not naturally break the law, and it attempts to stay compatible with human aspects as much as possible. However, once it exceeds the strategic limits of ethical profitability, it will clearly become a negative action. This misrepresentation that hides a lot of deception would ask people to bite off more than they can chew, and this is not one of the ethics of positive lying and is not related to it in any way.

In this way, marketing can become unethical for two reasons. We are responsible for the first one, while managements that run misleading and inhumane marketing activities are responsible for the other one. Commercial positive lying must be seen as a professional marketing tool that we can find wherever we go, so that we do not allow ourselves to be wasteful or to fall victims to insignificant things that we do not need. Once we become aware of these strategies, not only will we prevent ourselves from wasting our money, but we will also be able to differentiate between those who are trying to violate ethical limits and those who are following the law. Look at this positive lying from its creative and bright side and ignore the negative aspects that are likely to affect us, either because of us or because of others.

The Most Powerful Widespread Positive Lies

'Many of the things that we rely on in our lives and seek to obtain are just innovations that serve our interests or lies that regulate our lives and highlight the differences between us. Just as deceit can be lethal, it can also be a saviour if it was concerned with the public interest.'

'One of the positive lying facts.'

We will not just mention these usual positive lies because there are other forms that are more common than those social positive lies. The most powerful widespread positive lies are another form of positive lying. Usual forms of positive lying are just social skills. As for the most powerful positive lies, they are tangible inventions, habits and rules that we have been committed to. Their goal is to try to find more sophisticated civilisations that rely on combining science and entertainment, to make us ultimately people who master their work with high professionalism and live an organised life.

In short, most useful things that we have invented can be considered positive lies because they are subject to change, modification or even elimination. The ideas that people have come up with through history are not fixed conceptions that are presented to us by the universe like nature and religions, which are difficult to tamper with or even to distort slightly. The following positive lies will further explain this.

Lie # 1: **Money**. It might be a bit annoying that money has become among the most powerful positive lies of our time. Perhaps this was not the case before. In the past, currency consisted of gold, silver, bronze and other things that can be considered real currencies. The money we are talking about here is paper money or paper notes. It is not valuable in itself, but we have invented it and assigned value to it.

How can money not be a real thing even though we spend many years running after it? That is a truth no one wants to know about. However, if money is not something real, it is then a positive lie with real benefits. The value of something cannot be determined only by what is apparent, but by the tangible results it has in our lives.

Look at a hundred dollar note (or any other currency) and another one worth one dollar and try to find an actual difference between them. The difference is only in the colours and the writing on them. Alternatively, try to print a one hundred dollar note and another worth one dollar and you will find that they will have the same cost. It is almost the same note, and what makes it different is what is written on it and the size which is probably a bit smaller or bigger.

Paper money is one of the most beneficial positive lies that has been used throughout ages, because it has helped facilitate our lives, and has made countries have a good, or at least acceptable, economy. Without these invented currencies, money would have been something very difficult to obtain. The era in which we live now, regardless of all its disadvantages and crises, is indeed one of the best and most advanced. The easy life we live now has not been experienced by those who lived a few centuries ago, not to mention millions of years ago, when people did not see the light and most of what is now available. Currency notes have had a great influence in the development that happened and the things that they have made easier in our lives are invaluable.

You may see that at a time when the economy of a country collapses, the value of currency drops and loses its former status, all in accordance with the specific laws. Whereas gold and other natural and real minerals retain their value. The drawings and colours you see on the paper money have nothing to do with their value; their value is determined according to specific studies and policies. When we see that the value of the paper currency in a country corresponds to the value of the gold it owns, that indicates that the paper currency is nothing but a positive lie because gold is real and has a fixed value. The goal is generally to facilitate everything related to money. If money was made of gold, silver or any other real metal as it used to be in the past, life would not be as easy as it is now. Since metal is rare and difficult to attain, it would not be reasonable to spend it in exchange for bread.

Because metals are rare they can be easily seized by a few people, compared to the world population. Few people would have lived in luxury and the majority would have lived in poverty. The metals that were previously used as currency are natural and difficult to extract. If we ran out of them, it would not be possible to manufacture more of them. If currency still used those natural metals, only a few would be able to get it, compared with the population we share this life with. As for the paper currency we can produce as much as we want, endlessly. Since the source of currency notes can be controlled, we can make a lot of it. Thus, there will be no fear for the future of individuals as we used to have before the advent of paper currency.

'The US dollar is the most powerful currency in the world not because of its shape, size or the difficulty of forging it or for being a real metal; but because it has enough of the real thing - gold - to protect it.'
'One of the positive lying facts.'

Moreover, one of the advantages of paper currency is that it can carry and transfer the cultures of countries, the people and their heritage or history. Currencies show images of kings or presidents as well as cities that have a noteworthy history. Keep in mind that there are countries that were destroyed by wars. Their currency is no longer valuable. If currency used something real, such as gold for example, its value would not have dropped or been affected by wars or crises around it. Therefore, you can see how a note that used to be worth a lot one day is not worth a penny today, despite being the same piece of paper and nothing has changed about it.

A paper note is not something that has real value, it is simply paper. The reason for its remarkable value is those glistening, shiny metals, which would never lose value even with the passage of time. This innovative lie may make us believe that positive lying is a powerful force for innovation and creativity, and that it always aims at helping simplify people's lives. If we dare to imagine that there was no paper money we would feel so terrible, and it would be terrifying to even imagine or think of a situation like that.

Positive Lie # 2: **Your Name**. Names are unchangeable titles; they are formal and positive titles. Your name was the guesswork of two people - your parents - who were suggesting names to each other, calling you names in a speculative way and trying to stick to one of them. Whatever your name is, it came through guesswork or perhaps by chance, in order to distinguish you from others.

We can ask, what would happen if someone changed their name to another name? As for what people will do, nothing will happen except that they will change the name they were using to call that person; they will change his name to the new one he has chosen. More importantly, what will happen to this man on the personal level? Nothing will change other than that the letters of his name, which was written and approved in the records of others. As for his appearance, intelligence and everything else, they will all remain the same.

'People give themselves names in the same way they name their pets. In both cases, the names are invented, and they do not reflect a cosmic truth.'

'One of the positive lying facts.'

The names that people give to animals are like the names they give to their children; they are not real names, they are just creative titles. The name you gave to your pet was not its real name, but you chose it for it in order to distinguish it and to make dealing with it easier. If we could give ourselves the name we wanted at the moment of our birth, we would probably have identified ourselves with names other than those we now carry.

As we can see, no one was born with a specific name stamped on his forehead. It is not an innate matter but an innovation worthy of our human nature. The issue has its own dimensions and it is not even necessary to take it too seriously. Names in short, hold an aesthetic aspect, and most importantly they give us the ability to distinguish individuals and keep special records of them.

Lie # 3: **Your country / your origin**. Human beings are simply a mixture of different intellectual systems and cultures, and the person we were born as does not reflect who we really are; that is, the origin we were destined to have does not have to reflect who we are or what corresponds best with our real personalities. Although this disparity may not seem understandable to some, it gives fair judgement and is not intended to distinguish between the competencies of people from different origins.

This issue is not definitively final. If we combined people from different origins in a certain environment within a culture that is distinctive from their home cultures, they would form a harmonious mixture and would come up with new ideas. We would also notice that they would agree on how to live.

Therefore, origins reflect a particular cultural circle of some societies; they do not reflect a universal issue but rather social rules distinguishing different people from one another. These rules can be modified and reordered in infinite ways. It has become clear to us how easy it is to change our origin once we leave our original home countries. We stop relying on the culture of the old country, and we embrace new cultures that unite us with new people living there.

'One's origin is somehow similar to the phrase, 'Made in'. In both cases, we care about the quality not the place, be it a man or a thing. But quality here refers to the quality of the systems of thought that came with the product.'

'One of the positive lying facts.'

Loyalty to one's country is merely a positive lie that has its own cons and pros. When someone migrates to a new country or when he lives there for long periods of time, they start to feel at home and to have a new origin. The matter is simply no more than identifying one's identity, and this identity can be modified and changed for the better. On the other hand, one's origin refers simply to the acquisition of a particular culture, just like names, and in most cases this culture is similarly subject to change and replacement.

Positive Lie # 4: **Uniforms**. Formal clothes are one of the well-thought out positive lies that seek to achieve many public benefits. Wearing formal clothes is a widespread positive lie that has become increasingly reliable in the last few decades, due to the big developments in culture and technology. There is hardly ever any school, company or profession that does not require wearing uniforms. Many governments and official circles have come up with a certain formal uniform in order to distinguish themselves from others and to enhance the quality of their workplace.

If we asked a pilot to wear the uniform of a police officer on his next trip, how would he feel? Would it affect his performance? Uniforms are not merely for appearance only. There are other psychological implications involved. Our performance can improve or become worse depending on what we are wearing.

Good performance in official places does not only depend on organisational or scientific factors. What we wear at workplaces is not a matter of appearance because everything we wear can affect our psychologies. If a police officer wore the uniform of a pilot, his performance would deteriorate and he would lose the confidence that he used to have when he used to wear his usual formal uniform.

This actually encourages order and increases practical efficiency without having to be aware of it; it is an issue of encouragement based on indirect strategies. Uniforms that people have to wear in different companies, governments and schools etc. have been designed in line with the public interest, in order to ensure a high level of confidence and psychological support for better performance.

When we wear a uniform of a certain profession, we feel as if we have become part of that profession. If we wore the uniform of a chef, we would feel as if we were part of that profession. If we wore the uniform of a pilot, we would pretend to be skilled pilots. This applies to any other profession or type of official work.

This explains some of the issues that are hard to express in words. At the same time, uniforms do not only have the advantage of making people look good, they also give a sense of elegance. The goal is to add value that combines a sense of merit and trust, with a sense of elegance and good appearance and this would generate a sense of strength and mastery.

Positive Lie # 5: **Birthdays**. Birthdays are not real holidays. They simply reflect a happy memory. Birthdays may have advantages and disadvantages. This means that they can be considered as positive lies at certain times and negative at others. These parties are usually held to show gratitude for the gift of life that we were given. Nevertheless, before we celebrate our birthdays, we have to ask ourselves, 'What have we given the world that would make our birthday a happy occasion for us, as well as for others? Do we really deserve to celebrate this day?' Many celebrate their birthdays when in fact it represents more of a curse than a happy memory.

Celebrating our birthdays might act as a reminder of the fact that we have come one step closer to running out of years. It can remind us that the years we are destined to live are gradually decreasing. Then, that day would not seem a happy day after all. Birthdays are like alarms that warn us once a year, in order to review what we have achieved personally and with regard to others in the period that has passed.

'Every time we give the world something valuable, we have a new birthday. As for the regular birthdays, they merely express our gratitude to the gift of life that we possess.'

'One of the positive lying facts.'

Our birthdays do not necessarily have to occur once a year. Every moment that passes with something beneficial we offer to the world, is a new birthday and a true, happy memory. When we celebrate our existence without first attempting to discover or seek out our goal in life and without giving any help or trying to benefit those around us, we seem to be celebrating the fact that our time is running out and death has come nearer.

Lie # 6: **Cinematic Acting**. It is the biggest entertaining positive lie. It is characterised by a wild imagination and creativity. Acting does not represent something real. It is more of a fantasy that does not exist, and often its purpose is to reverse reality. Playing characters of some well-known ancient figures or imitating the culture and work of other people might be useful and significant.

This kind of art did not use to be so prevalent in the recent past. However, modern times have helped influence a lot of creativity. This art has many positive aims, and it can be used to benefit people in many different ways. It is often intended to entertain people with imaginary stories and events that are visual. These stories can be funny or horrifying. It is also used for educational purposes and it can be one of the most successful teaching methods. We actually see this become more common in educational institutions. When our eyes perceive something, the mind becomes more capable of understanding it and the heart more capable of feeling it. Therefore, reading and listening may not be sufficient sometimes, without moving pictures that would help us feel what we see and understand it more deeply.

Thanks to this positive lie, we can turn the past into present, and illusion into a visible fact. The transition between ages, planets, galaxies and seeing and hearing the voice of people in the past who were never seen or heard by anyone, has become easy and fun too. Acting may not be real, but it can show us clearly how certain individuals, peoples and countries used to live.

Perhaps we need some clarification on how acting reflects reality not facts. There is a great similarity between the two. It is true that when we watch a film, we may see real things and events, but these events might not have happened. It is possible to say that every truth is real. However, not every reality is true. Reality can change or be modified in order to achieve many different goals, but truth is fixed - no one can tamper with it or attempt to change it.

If you saw Paul Walker's great driving skills in his movies, you would realise that he was trying to portray a fun and daring reality. However, attempting to make this true in real life can be deadly. Truths cannot be modified and challenging them can pose serious danger on us.

This is similar to what happened with Christopher Reeve, who is a superhero. It seemed illogical for him to become paralysed after being thrown from a horse in one of the equestrian competitions. An accident like this can happen to a hero in the actual world, whereas in the reality based on positive lying this accident cannot happen.

In the end, be a brilliant actor. Not in cinemas but in the reality you live. Since your acting seeks to please people, deepen their love for you, eliminate their fears or to achieve any other positive purposes, this still will not pose any danger to you or anyone else.

The Biggest Negative Lies in the World: Sad Jokes

'It is quite shameful for a creature with wisdom and the ability to think consciously and logically to believe whatever he sees or hears, without giving himself time to use his ability to first analyse and interpret, instead of following irrational feelings and fantasies.'
'One of the Smart Discrediting facts.'

Negative lies you will face are not a reflection of personal opinions, and they are far from being biased; they rather reflect logic and truth. We often hear about many things and believe most of what we hear. These lies are the biggest negative lies that the world came up with, and without which there are no tangible benefits. They are jokes covered with seriousness, and this is why we take them more seriously than they are worth. An invented lie will not become positive if there are no real benefits to it and positive goals for its creation.

There are many negative lies around the world, but not all of them deserve to be mentioned here because they are considered relatively small, and they do not cause much harm to our lives. However, these big lies are great and fateful. They have manipulated people's lives and pushed them towards negativity and superstition. Such lies changed people's behaviour and actions so that they became less dependent on their conscious actions. Eventually, the lies made people believe in luck instead of relying on themselves and waiting for results without taking the means leading to them.

Positive lies are positive because they give you an opportunity to use them positively, and people often get help from them in many different life situations. However, negative lies are negative and have nothing beneficial in them and history proves that. They include practical lies, academic lies, religious lies and others. Our imagination and ignorance are the source of these lies. They are based on foundations that have no useful purposes, and some of these lies do not even have a foundation. Our aim here is not to undermine the efforts of others, deny and rebel against natural laws or question our religions, but to have a more creative and realistic life.

Negative Lie # 1: **Daily horoscopes**. We have learned from our wisest minds that happiness and success come from one source: our thinking and our conscious effort. It is unwise to listen to predictions and guesses about who we are, how our day will be, where we will get our source of income, how much happiness we will have, what kind of achievements we will achieve, the quality of our relationships or the success we will achieve in our lives. The ones who believe these lies or listen to them are lost in this life. If anyone is going to determine who we are and what we will get in life, it is better to be us with our conscious efforts and no one else. Freedom of choice lies in our hands and will always be available to us.

It is unrealistic for a person appearing on a screen or a newspaper story to determine the quality of the life one will live. Naturally, everything we have now and everything we will get in the future is of our own choice and the result of our hard work, not the result of those horoscopes - or predictions - that are far from reality.

Unfortunately, many still listen to these tips and believe what they tell them; some wake up and listen to horoscopes first thing in the morning in order to see how their day will go socially, emotionally and financially. Then they would take action accordingly. For example, if their day is supposed to give them a 50% success rate on the emotional or social side, they will act accordingly, because they have programmed themselves and their brains to have a relationship quality that does not exceed that specified percentage. In fact, everything would have been much better if they had not heard or read that information that is far from the truth.

'Nothing has the ability to determine how much success we can get in our day but ourselves. Horoscopes are nothing but a daily game that was invented for those who are lost and who do not have a sense of their own selves anymore. They are also furthest from being real.'

'One of the Smart Discrediting facts.'

The worst trick we could fall victim to is when someone tells us what we might do or get in our day and future life in general. Still, is it possible to use horoscopes in a positive way? In any case, it is preferable to get rid of them. If you want to rely on your horoscope, the first thing you have to do is stop listening to the news it brings you. Instead of listening to them, try to determine what your horoscope will say for you. In doing so, expect that the expectations you set for yourself will happen at possibility no less than 90 %, and you can live your day in all its aspects according to that percentage.

Horoscopes fall within the domain of astrologers, and astrology is a negative lie, used and relied on in ancient times. However, now we are living in wiser and more developed times. If you think you need some astrologers to give you glimpses of your future, be that astrologer and promise yourself that you will be the sole controller of your destiny. Your faults do not necessarily have to indicate weakness or failure; they are simply normal circumstances that happen to almost everyone.

Negative Lie # 2: **The image of Christ**. We are not sure of the source of the image of the prophet Jesus, but what is certain is that we see in our mind a loving and peace-loving messenger. Truth will still be the truth, whether we spread it or hide it, love it or hate it and whether we like it or not. In fact, it will not matter much to us to know the painter of the image, and we do not want to look long into ancient history. However, we will examine some points that may help in determining the validity of the image.

What would happen if after you wrote and published a book, people thanked and praised someone else? That must be very painful even to imagine, regardless of what you have accomplished. The image of Jesus is something similar. We are actually thanking and praising someone we do not know.

If you examine the history of that image, you will find that there are several different images and modifications of the image itself. As far as we know, people do not change considerably in appearance while they are alive, but what makes a man who is dead or unseen by us change in appearance? This explains to us the actual source of those images, which is the imagination of some painters. If we are to assume that his image is real, then why aren't there other images of other prophets? Painters have been around for almost all ages and even the worst painters can draw to us some of the features of the human face.

A forensic doctor named Richard Niv has conducted some studies that aim at highlighting the facial form that prevailed in the days of Christ. To do so, he tried to look into some of the faces that existed in his time as evidence. The results showed that there were no similar faces to the one in the picture at that time. In fact, there was a clear contradiction in the hair, skin colour and facial features between old images and the current image. It was found that his hair was not long and soft, but a little short and wrinkled, and that the colour of his skin was a little brown with a little red, and his eyes were relatively dark. Proof of this can be found in the words of other messengers and those who lived in his time. What they described is very similar to what the study showed.

That evidence contained simply an inaccurate description of a figure whose details we do not yet know. Actually, we are capable of seeing the prophet Jesus without the need of any description or image. We see him as a great man who blesses any place he enters. Keep in mind that this issue is about faith and faith does not need any images. It rather requires a strong heart that can believe in divine miracles.

Negative Lie # 3: **A certificate can guarantee that you'll find work and money**. Everything we do in life must have a goal. Without a goal in mind our actions have no value, even though they involve valuable things. When it comes to having a certificate, we have first to identify a goal behind getting this certificate. If we do not find one, there might not be a need for it.

It is estimated that the time it took us to develop from old and primitive times does not exceed one hundred years, and university disciplines have a clear and effective role in this transition. If we went back in time, only about fifty years to the late 20th century, we would recognise very little of the development we see in the world now. This shows the great speed we have developed at thanks to the different specialties and disciplines and their fair distribution.

Therefore, we are not talking here about the science that is taught, but how university degrees can determine the type of work and the amount of money we can get. In fact, there is an unfair correlation between academic science and the money we will earn, as well as the quality of our jobs. Many people work in similar fields, but these fields have clear material and moral differences. You might find a doctor who is rich and happy with his work and another doctor who is poor and hates his job, and this applies to all other fields of work.

We all receive similar certificates and we definitely get different grades or marks. However, the majority do not see that. They think that the certificates that everyone seems to get are the same and that the money and work we will have after we receive them, will grant us an independent life financially, which would allow us to do whatever we like. The difference is that what we get will represent different experiences based on our nature. Every human being has his own experiences, visions and goals. If anyone is going to bring us money and a good job then that had better be ourselves, by knowing who we are and identifying our natural capabilities and by understanding the nature of money and how to earn it.

That unfair correlation is making those who chose to stay away from the academic world realise that they do not have a chance of a successful future or even have more than they need for living. As this notion became more common, one might start to wonder if he would ever reach advanced stages in his work or achieve financial success. This has become a well-known fact that is undeniable for most people.

The statement that says, 'A certificate guarantees you get work and money,' reminds us of a similar saying we have, 'Any type of work is not shameful.'. This statement is the reason why our efforts are lost in useless jobs we do because we convince ourselves that 'any type of work is not shameful,' and these useless jobs have been made to look heroic. We understand the harsh conditions that force one to work anywhere and do anything to secure basic needs. The circumstances that compel us to do certain jobs that do not suit us, are not as cruel as the ones that keep us from getting education in order to get basic needs. The man who does not mind what he does or where he works, is someone confused and lost because he does not know himself well nor the destination he seeks to reach. What is shameful to a person is when he does not take advantage of his great potential, but instead looks to find something to eat. That only fits creatures that do not have reason.

This lie was invented because of the fear of poverty and the lack of self-awareness. The fear of having little money makes one look for safe ways to get money such as long-term employment because it provides a steady income. Not knowing yourself means not having a deep sense of who you are and consequently not knowing the best job for you.

There are many contradictions here. We see many people who secure good lives because of their degrees, but who start to whine and grumble when they move to practical life. They are uncomfortable in what they are doing, and they do not earn enough money to make themselves happy. The paradox here is that if you want to become rich, why would you go and spend long years studying medicine? There is no connection between getting a lot of money and studying medicine or accounting. There is no subject or course in school or a major at college that can teach you how to become rich. On the other hand, there are many rich people who know very well about these special courses or disciplines and love to make them public so others can learn them too

We do not work to pay bills and buy food, but to add value and real creativity to our world. The difference is that when you work to meet your everyday needs, you will spend your life working without clear goals and you will not get results in the end. When you live to work, you will play roles that you have chosen for yourself not for others, and the results you will eventually get will be more than mere material rewards. Therefore, you have the freedom to choose either to be preoccupied with the results or preoccupied with the work.

The famous actor, Rowan Atkinson, had finished his studies at the University of Oxford in the field of electrical engineering, yet he insisted on playing a completely different role in life, in the field of acting. As did the philosopher of pragmatism William James who has a degree in medicine but was known as a founder of psychology and a philosopher, although his real specialty is medicine. This offers a good lesson to those who draw limits to their lives because they do not have a higher degree. Nothing can prevent us from doing what we love.

'Work is the machine that continues to invent all that is valuable for the future of humanity. Money is among the innovations that have been found to reward us if we complete our work honestly and with dedication. A degree is not the power that makes a machine work; it is just an innovation and a tool for organising work. Disbelieve in the wrong ways of using it, in order to find the best job and increase your income.'

'One of the Smart Discrediting facts.'

There are many creative jobs and if we rely on a tool with limited possibilities, we will lose a large part of our ability to search for the most creative jobs that are in line with our personalities. That tool does not need much effort to get or to use. A creative role does not care about the adopted laws and is not confined within limited strategies. It just needs effort while looking for it and then hard work in trying to bring it to existence with the available tools. If we abandon this role relying on a particular discipline, we will lose the courage to move further away from that safe and well-known zone, through which we can create captivating scenes that the world has have never seen before.

Negative Lie # 4: **Have a leader**. Some may mix between having a leader and having a role model, who is an example you follow; a person who influences your behaviour and whose actions and creative ideas affect you. Making someone your leader means you imitate their behaviour, whether negative or positive. However, having a role model means you take the positive behaviours and beliefs of someone and transfer them to you, while avoiding negative and harmful behaviour. All of this happens voluntarily on your part. This makes it one of the worst negative lies that people have believed and that are widely spread in almost all societies, because it makes people focus on results instead of causes.

When we have a leader, it means we have accepted to have someone dominating us. Therefore, we would lose the ability to differentiate between wrong and right. A leader is a person who makes our decisions for us, controls our thinking and directs our paths and therefore our destiny. Relying on someone completely is like being inside a video game leaving someone else in control. There are many people who follow irresponsible leaders, who make unconscious decisions for them and who have a negative or hypocritical mentality.

That person can be your father, your manager or even your country's president. When you allow someone to make decisions for you and impose on you roles that do not match your mentality and potential, you will prevent yourself from developing and make your life controlled by someone else. On the other hand, people learn from their role model positive things only and they have the freedom to take what they want and leave what they don't. This is what he wants too.

No leader will understand you as much as you understand yourself, but you first need continuous learning in order for you to gain comprehensive knowledge. Achieving this requires skilled leaders who have already discovered their own selves. These leaders would constitute the starting point to discovering the leader inside you because, wishing for knowledge is not enough to gain knowledge.

'One of the Smart Discrediting facts.'

'Your father does not have to be your superior.' Fathers always give their children advice and tell them stories and ideas about different things in life, but that advice is only good if fathers have what they are preaching about. For example, it is not reasonable to take financial advice from your father if he is poor, advice on good health if his body is full of diseases or family and social advice if he does not have good and strong relations with others.

Fathers often wish their children everything good in life and they always give them a lot of advice. A father always tells his son, 'I want you to become rich. I want you to be better than me.' Then he gives him tips and lessons to live the life he had always dreamed of but did not achieve because he had little knowledge.

The first case (wishing you to be rich) is possible; he does want you to be rich, but the second (giving you his own advice) is almost always not true. The advice he will give you will lead you to the same difficult road he took. It is simply a matter of different expressions. If he has worked as a regular employee all his life and wants you to work in a better field to get more money, he will not guide you to investments and teach you the necessary skills. He will rather convince you to have the same field because it is the only thing he knows about and if he deviates from his lifestyle, he will change nothing of what you will get at the end. As you know, people cannot talk about things they do not know or that they have not learned before.

Fathers often destroy the lives of their children indirectly, believing that they are helping them with their knowledge and long experience because they do not know their children well. You might wonder how it is possible for a father not to know his children, and that is quite logical. It might also sound strange when someone says that their close friends know them better than their fathers do, or that they know their friends better than their own parents do. Unfortunately, nowadays fathers and their sons do not know each other anymore.

Knowing someone does not mean knowing his name, the places he likes to go to or his favourite food. It is knowing his true potential, his thoughts and his passion. Therefore, fathers' advice is often not considered or thought about well. It is merely based on previous beliefs. Fear makes fathers give their children emotional advice that is not based on reason. Your father gives you advice based on what he thinks and believes to be the best, instead of considering what is best for you.

Some people might have a good knowledge of something, but they have not used it. That's true, but how do you guarantee that? These people are only a few and those who have knowledge about things that are really valuable but do not use that knowledge, are often not eager to learn and have a poor memory.

If you decide one day to make your father your role model first think of what he has, of what he wants to give you. If he is giving you financial advice, look first at his bank account. If he is giving you social advice, look at his relationships and if he is giving you health advice, look at his health and ask him to show you the number of medicines he is taking. If you think you know the secret of happiness and want to teach it to others, first look at your happiness. If you are not happy, your thoughts will be wrong because if you had happiness you would have benefited yourself from it. Do not forget that the good intentions of your father towards you will not hide the harm that will befall you if you are doing what is wrong.

Do not make your manager your superior; make him your biggest supporter. You will find many at work who are higher than you in rank and who impose rules on you that you have to follow. Here you have to look inside you. In other words, you have to change your views and attitude before you look at others. Those who do not develop and rise at work do not see themselves as deserving of the best; they are even incapable of imagining the best happening to them. They actually see those who are higher than them, as mighty people who are difficult to reach. In this case, those thoughts will be sent to the brain so that it reprograms itself and remains the same.

The idea here is not about having respect for those who are higher than you, nor is it about loving or hating them. This is rather about loving and respecting yourself. He who loves himself will never accept to remain the same with no change and will not let others control him. When you look at those who are higher than you at work as a source of help, you will benefit from them. If they do not have anything to offer, then at least you will not care if they annoy or harass you and this is quite useful.

At work, the words of those who are higher than you may sound like orders and not accepting them means, often, the end of your career. What you should do is accept those words but keep being creative on the inside, without letting anyone feel that until the time is right to reveal your creativity. If you do that, you will rise up until you reach high levels that you used to think were difficult to attain. What we have to understand is that we have to follow the laws and rules in our practical lives, but not with the mentality of those who view everyone as being more valuable than them and will remain so. You need to see your own rules as a reality one day. The more you know yourself the more valuable your ideas become and the more valuable you become. How great you see yourself will determine how others will see you. Exaggerating the status of others will hinder you from seeing your actual value in the present and future.

Your country ruler does not have to be your superior. For many societies, the ruler of the state is often like a saviour who will make people's lives easy and enjoyable. The ruler of any society is a highly empowered employee, and nothing more. However, some rulers may become greedy because some unethical powers are given to them. Entrusting someone with your life and letting them control it is something that hastens the destruction of your future. The ruler of your country is not much different from your boss or father or anyone else who might control your life. What makes it worth mentioning is that you see many depend on their rulers, whether prince, president or king, as if he is the one who will make their lives better and happier. They would often forget that they are the true masters of themselves and their lives.

Nowadays, if you look at the poorest and most corrupt societies in the world, you will find that they have entrusted their lives to their rulers without considering their own views. Those societies have lost their sense of responsibility and of continuous self-improvement. When you depend on someone blindly you become servile. When you allow a political regime to control you, you unconsciously become a slave.

However, if we look at those powerful and advanced societies that give to life more than just new babies, you will see that they are free and unrestricted by political systems. Their societies are full of individuals who bear responsibility and do not allow anyone to control them and make decisions on their behalf. They always aspire to new things. Once you free yourself from the constraints of others, you recognise yourself and you look at it before you look at others. The blind pursuit of anyone without any freedom of choice is the primary reason behind the destruction of individuals and societies.

Negative Lie # 5: **Interest loans**. In commercial positive lying, we are completely free of any obligations or restrictions. We simply have nice offers trying to add joy to our hearts. However, when it comes to interest loans that claim to help people and meet their needs, they are not only negative but also one of the most inhumane acts. The reason is that they make people live a restricted and difficult life which deprives them of living a free life. Loads of debts make life complicated and disgraceful.

Commercial areas have expanded to include more than providing a valuable product or service that benefit people for money. This expansion does not mean that such businesses follow positive and humanitarian methods. Many business practices have breached ethical barriers to profit and have moved to a stage where people are obliged to pay their money compulsively to those who do not deserve it, sometimes answering serious merciless threat.

This is not about debt. Debt is acceptable if it aims to help people personally, without any intermediaries or strict banking transactions. When we fall victim to an interest loan it is not about debt, but about serious restrictions that will endanger our lives and property. At any moment, we can become bankrupt and our property might get confiscated after we have worked hard for years to get it.

Interest loans are not good things that help people as it is commonly known. Such loans encourage people to bear more than they can and place them in critical financial positions. This has caused people to live a material life running behind money for fear of losing it.

'Own a house without an asset' is the slogan that many banks use in their ads. The truth is that the asset is under their control, and at any time they can destroy everything that you have been trying to build for years if you do not pay them what is not actually their right.

The thing that contributed most to the success of this idea is that people do not have prior knowledge of the nature of money. They do not know about ways to invest it. They only want a lot of money without the need to work for it for years. Getting a loan, therefore, seems an easier option than working hard and waiting for years to buy a certain house or car. Little knowledge and little patience distract careful planning processes and make people pursue every idea that can potentially make their dreams true or that can bring them what they want in a short period of time. It is fine to deduct half of the income we are currently getting. We have come a long way towards the future we wanted.

The problem lies in the possibilities that we do not expect and never plan for. What we are borrowing money for requires large expenses too. The income we are sure of getting might stop before those many years that we need to pay the loan back have passed. Worst of all, we will live a very complicated and restricted life, so greed becomes obvious in our actions for fear of losing the money we must give to those who do not deserve it.

The lack of the right balance in the fair distribution of funds is the fundamental problem. The real humanitarian aid that we have to provide are being lost. Instead, people are giving their money to those who do not deserve it, not to the needy.

If we look carefully at all the money that is due to banks, we find that it is an inverted, unbalanced or unfair process since the poor here is the one who is giving money to the rich, not the other way around. It is not about repaying the money borrowed by the poor but about that heavy interest, which is more important to pay than the loan itself. This injustice is the result of keeping money in the hands of those who do not need it, with apparently positive ways that don't break international laws.

We will be happy to help everyone in need. That is one of our human qualities. However, while we are inundated with great debts and commitments, we will prevent ourselves from giving the needy and we will deprive ourselves and others of fair support. Instead, we will be living through difficult lifestyles; living a life in which we are running after a banknote, always fearing losing our mortgaged property to others. That is the worst and most pathetic form of life.

We may not be able to prevent such practices in the era of speed in which we live now. The idea of working dozens of months to own a house is no longer logical but getting a house after spending a few minutes signing a loan transaction will be much easier and faster as it does not need a lot of thinking.

However, in the end we follow a path that seems to be embellished from the outside, but when we take that path we will see how it is monstrous and merciless. At first, we were free but as soon as we entrusted ourselves to others, we started to be overwhelmed. Any violation of the laws would cost us a lot. So, remember not to associate yourself with debt and heavy commitments, and live a free life where no one is expecting anything from you.

Negative Lie # 6: **Reading palms and cups**. We still see many of those who read palms or cups as if what they see are real visions or divine messages. This foolishness is similar to horoscopes, but it is hidden in a different form.

Whoever practices acts like these are people who do not feel secure and who have no goals to achieve. A sane person will not possibly believe in senseless drawings in an empty cup, nor will he allow someone to predict his future by looking at natural curves in his hands. Only those who do not believe in being the only ones deciding their own fate will surely love that.

Similar to the lies in horoscopes, if there is one thing that is capable of determining our future, it is our conscious thinking and our sincere efforts, not cups, palms or horoscopes. Those who believe in themselves, in their mind's capabilities and in their ability to plan their own future with their own actions, do not need to believe in these negative and unrealistic ideas.

Even if some people have pleasure in these things or view them as things that make them enthusiastic and optimistic, they should know that they can get all of this through positive lying; we are able to convince ourselves and imagine doing everything we wish for and believe in that without any external help. When you encourage yourself and set goals, it is better and safer if you seek these goals without help from curves in palms or drawings in dirty cups. At that moment, you would have chosen the roles that deserve working for and you would have chosen what you want eventually. In fact, when we accept the fake external help from those predictions, even when they bring us good news, most probably they will not be in line with our best efforts because at the end they will be mere unnecessary speculations.

Negative Lie # 7: **Customs and Traditions**. By following customs and traditions we remain limited within a certain intellectual level, with no change or development which makes them more of an intellectual prison that we can lock ourselves into. When we hold on to beliefs for too long, or perhaps for a whole lifetime, we deprive ourselves from many new ideas, customs and other things that are more valuable. Customs and traditions are usually invented by small groups of people, so they are valid only for a small number of people.

In every time, there are different traditions, lifestyles and ways of thinking because we have a lot of different people who are trying to invent useful things to the world, without clinging to old ways of life and to old and limited ways of thinking. Old traditions only become old when we come up with new things and those new things will in turn, become old when we come up with what is even newer and this chain is endless. Customs and traditions that many communities still hold on to are ways through which those communities express their desire of survival and adherence to all that is old.

We are different and each person has his or her own creative capabilities and ways of thinking, but how can we become different or come up with new ideas if we all adhere to fixed and limited beliefs and ways of thinking? There are many fixed things that most people hold on to and these things do not have to change regardless of the passage of time. Despite all the changes and development we witness throughout ages, we will not possibly come up with things that prevent us from having intercourse, praying, eating or drinking. These are natural principles in life and what makes them different is that they were created by the Creator. As for different customs and traditions, they were invented by someone whose time has passed and expired.

People may interpret your departure from their traditions as rebellious or disrespectful actions and this may hurt those who seek to excel in a new way. The best thing to do here is to embrace their traditions, but only in front of them. When you are alone practice new things that you see as unique and effective. Few people will understand your new philosophy and many of them will regard it as a rebellion against their practices. There is no need to explain your new ideas or justify leaving the path that many had taken before you. Just nod, smile and keep those dangerous thoughts in your mind and do them only with those who understand you and see your individuality and appreciate it.

Customs and traditions, however fair they may be are not compatible with every human being. They often impose themselves on us without taking into account our opinion. Even when the things we are forced to follow were true or positive they will shortly have negative repercussions on our lives, because they did not give us enough space to express our ideas. Moreover, if we do not have enough knowledge of the positive things we do, i.e. the scientific interpretation for their existence, then we will not be able to keep them a long time because other things will take their place; things that fall under our control and within our own interpretation.

The number of those who fall victim to this negative lie remains very high, and many have abandoned healthier and more creative ways of living and have been forced to practice the methods imposed on them as the best and safest ways. Imitators are actually enemies of creativity and of every new and useful thing. They are usually unproductive and unhealthy; therefore, staying away from them is one of the best favours you can do for yourself. So, learn something new in the morning of every new day and do not imitate anyone or follow their steps no matter how great they were. Identify the best values and principles that correspond to your nature and talents. By doing so, you become the best person you can be.

Negative Lie # 8: **Mixing the world of Jinn and the world of Mankind**. Throughout history, many myths have been hidden under the cover of truth. The stories we have read, and the images shown on television have made these myths seem real, or perhaps have helped them be experienced by some individuals in certain places.

Just as water and oil will remain separate no matter how hard we try to mix them, the world of the Jinn will remain separated from our world, and there is no universal evidence that can prove that Jinn can enter the world of man or tamper with it. This is about limits that cannot be trespassed. We can see the truth of this matter if we look at certain sources of awareness, such as religions and the wisest minds that rely on their own studies and cosmic realities, to provide us with sufficient knowledge.

What seems true about these things is just fake news spread by those who are ignorant of the scientific and real interpretation of what they see. News channels show us events without giving us realistic explanations of what they are reporting. They report events as they are with a general and vague explanation of what is really happening.

Real-life events we witness are nothing more than acute mental illnesses. There are many mental disorders that call for incomprehensible or stable behaviours, and that clearly indicate madness and loss of reason. In the end, these stories are never about Jinn's interference in someone's life as that is something that can only happen in horror movies on screens, just for fun and making profit.

The danger lies in instilling fear in the hearts of those who might believe such things, so they end up living their lives in fear. Worse still, stories of Jinn can be associated with some diseases. Once some people are exposed to certain diseases, they think that the cause is a strange satanic touch and they start to act unconsciously as if that were true. Therefore, this becomes a mental and psychological encouragement that would worsen disease or bring about sickness, just like drugs that have negative side effects.

Negative Lie # 9: **Love is one form of feelings**. It is clear that the vast majority of people still rely on their hearts more than their conscious thinking which is supposed to create successful relationships that have mutual respect. Because of our lack of understanding of successful social norms and our failure to master them, we have begun to follow certain traditions that are not suited to the intelligent, social creature.

Many relationships break down mainly because we deal with them with feelings that are far from rationality and wisdom. Therefore, we only create emotional reactions that frustrate the continuity of the relationships we need. When we deal with anything with our feelings, we do this thing and ourselves an injustice. When we treat people with our feelings our relationship with them will not last long, and we will have many disputes. Moreover, we will focus on trivial rather than important things.

In relationships, we cannot take something without giving something first. It is not possible for others to give us what we have not asked for or at least hinted at. As for the more intimate relationships, the exchange of expectations may happen before marriage, but what happens next is that each side is forced to abandon their emotions and to resort to more rational and responsible things, and here lies the boring shock to many. This means that we are basically dealing with others using reason instead of emotions. The mind has flexibility and creativity that enable it to determine the appropriate reaction to any situation.

The best forms of love are those represented by friendship. Friendship may not be the same as love but if we maintain feelings of love and acts of friendship, we will form eternal relationships. Actions are always preceded by feelings and both are often linked to each other significantly. Moreover, those who control their feelings will be able to separate them from actions even for a short time. Friends always know how to preserve their feelings of love. Even when incidents confuse their relationship, they turn to reason and put emotions aside.

Friendships last longer because they are based on positive mental perceptions and rational actions, whereas the concept of love is based on emotional reactions so it often results in selfish behaviours, that do not understand or appreciate the other. Friendship does not allow feelings to raise negative doubts or fantasies.

The sacrifices we have seen from people who love each other have been based on real actions. Relationships based on rational initiatives usually last forever, as opposed to those based on feelings which rarely last for a long time and that usually end because of worthless and insignificant trifles. If our relationships did not have clear features, we would live with vague and unclear feelings.

Emotions are nothing more than direct self-reflection of what you think. Give priority to friendship and rationality to create familiarity and love between you and people, rather than waiting for these to come from others because more often such feelings will not come.

'One of the Smart Discrediting facts.'

Giving is the foundation upon which our relationships are based. The strongest relationships are those which maintain friendship and giving, without relying on emotions that undermine the role of reason. The quickest way to bring people and even animals together is through sincere giving. The most effective giving in relationships is not to give tangible things, but rather things that are intangible, such as attention, good words and a smile. Tangible things can have a temporary effect, but what you say and show continuously will determine the outcome.

In relationships, giving is represented by caring, trusting, forgiving and listening to the other side in order to see what they see. At this moment you leave yourself temporarily and start seeing with the other's eye and thinking with their mind. If you depart from yourself and allow your soul to enter the mind of the one you love, you will then find it easy to avoid long and selfish arguments. Having different opinions might be simply misunderstanding the other side. A deep understanding will lead you to cooperative solutions that satisfy all parties. By listening to people, trusting and respecting them, you will make yourself someone who cannot be abandoned or forgotten at least.

Negative Lie # 10: **The Antichrist**. Unbelievably, there are nearly two billion people who believed and still believe in the coming of a person called the Antichrist, most of whom are Muslims. It is said that his main goal is to spread corruption and play the role of God and possess great abilities: he can revive the dead, control nature by making the sky rain and the earth germinate; he has a paradise and a hell, in addition to other abilities.

Some may say that we do not have here enough evidence to prove this and that is right. However, the evidence here lies in the wisdom and logic that we can use to look at this.

Imagine that you spend decades building a house. After your long wait and your effort in building and renovating, you agree with people and paid them to destroy what you have worked hard to build for years. Do you see wisdom or logic in such an act? The Creator would be doing something similar if he would give of his abilities to a human being, or any other creature, to make people believe in that person and not believe in Him.

The number of messengers whom God sent to mankind is very great, and all this is to make people trust Him and His existence. When such a person is sent it will be like the one who demolishes his house after its construction. This is a great contradiction between words and deeds and reflects intentions that are not appropriate for divine wisdom.

Many people interpret this matter as a test from the Lord to measure how much people believe in Him. In fact, there is enough evidence to make people believe in His existence. The fact that people are alive might suffice to prove that. The presence of such a person is far from being interpreted as a test. The strongest believers will end up believing in a person who controls nature and brings the dead to life. It is not divine wisdom to create traps for people in order to spoil their lives and make them live an insecure life.

'Divine wisdom lies in creating systems that are compatible with human nature and its basic components to make us live a completed life from the spiritual, mental and physical aspects, not in making charlatans who seek to spread corruption among people.'
'One of the Smart Discrediting facts.'

What makes this lie so negative is that it shows how it will be followed by all humanity. The number of people who will not believe in him as a new god is only twenty thousand. This means that the number of people who will believe that they have a true god (not the Antichrist) among all those billions does not exceed twenty thousand, and the others will follow the Antichrist and believe in him. As for the speed with which he walks, he can cross the whole earth and all its cities in only forty days, riding a huge donkey. This is far from nature and physical laws, and even the fastest aircraft in the world will not be able to do something like that.

We have to understand that the number of charlatans now and in the old history is big enough to test people. Their goal has always been to push people to question their religions or to make them bad people who kill each other. Many of them were, and still are, trying to play the role of God, who breaks the rules of nature and seeks to make people believe in them as they believe in their God. Having someone like the Antichrist who possesses such divine abilities is illogical as there is no need for his arrival.

Proposals for The Application of Positive Lying

There are times when it is not wise to use positive lies. Positive lying can cause undesired disasters if we do not have a clear and realistic goal behind it. It is not wise to encourage someone to be strong enough to jump out of a building without getting hurt and this work is nothing more than an overly motivated action, that is void of clear goals and careful planning.

Therefore, positive lying does not mean that one should act recklessly and blindly. When you start using it either on yourself or others, you must first study the situation and plan well and in the long term. Positive lying is not just fleeting words. It needs prearranged plans and information that will precede action.

Using positive lying is not easy but it is not difficult. Through practice, you can use it more effectively and with greater flexibility. These are some suggestions that will make using positive lying easier and more secure.

1. Application of our ideas is more important than all the goals or information we have. There is no benefit from a

valuable idea that is not applied. So, make practical work an important step after lying to yourself directly and discrediting the other systems, to transform the purpose of the internal reality to a concrete external reality. The main obstacle is when you focus on results and neglect the methods. We are often happy to think about the results we will get, so we forget to focus on the ways that will lead us to the final result. This is a friendly trap that haunts most people and relies on bad mood and laziness, that make us shy away from sustained efforts towards a satisfactory outcome.

2. Do not over-lie to the point where you alienate yourself from reality. What we want to do must fall within our natural capacity so as not to drain us on the long run and take more time and effort than we can afford.

3. When you deem events or the words of others as lies, do not do that completely unless you benefit from what happened, because there may be important ideas that you can take into account and benefit from.

4. Do not overuse positive lying or involve it in all activities and businesses because there may be no need for it. Positive lying is a tool we use at certain times in which we need to motivate and remove fear from our hearts and its continuous use in our lives in all situations may be harmful. This overuse makes us overly question everything that is being said or done. This will only bring us anxiety about situations and events that do not require much concern.

5. Balance between lying to yourself and lying to others; do not make use of positive lying on the personal level only but use it to meet your interests and the interests of others.

6. Make sure not to combine positive and negative lying so that you do not lose one of its basic terms and conditions.

The best thing you can do is to create a table that clarifies the right use of the positive lie tool which would contain the situations and times when it is the right time to use it.

7. Use commercial lying to motivate and seduce others and make the product look its best. When the marketing or commercial methods we use are based on fraud in any way, we will be breaking the ethical rules of the profitability systems that commercial lying relies on. Commercial lying is not meant to be a burden on anyone. Moreover, it will lose its true meaning which seeks to benefit all parties, if we don't adhere to its ethical rules.